MAD LIBS®

PET PARADE MAD LIBS

MAD LIBS

An imprint of Penguin Random House LLC, New York

Pet Parade Mad Libs first published in the United States of America by Mad Libs,
an imprint of Penguin Random House LLC, New York, 2023

Visit us online at penguinrandomhouse.com.

Printed in the United States of America

Pet Parade Mad Libs ISBN 9780593521533
1 3 5 7 9 10 8 6 4 2
COMR

MAD LIBS

MEOW LIBS

by Sarah Fabiny

MAD LIBS®

INSTRUCTIONS

MAD LIBS® is a game for people who don't like games!
It can be played by one, two, three, four, or forty.

● RIDICULOUSLY SIMPLE DIRECTIONS

In this tablet you will find stories containing blank spaces where words are left out. One player, the READER, selects one of these stories. The READER does not tell anyone what the story is about. Instead, he/she asks the other players, the WRITERS, to give him/her words. These words are used to fill in the blank spaces in the story.

● TO PLAY

The READER asks each WRITER in turn to call out a word—an adjective or a noun or whatever the space calls for—and uses them to fill in the blank spaces in the story. The result is a MAD LIBS® game.

When the READER then reads the completed MAD LIBS® game to the other players, they will discover that they have written a story that is fantastic, screamingly funny, shocking, silly, crazy, or just plain dumb—depending upon which words each WRITER called out.

● EXAMPLE (*Before* and *After*)

"_____!" he said _____
  EXCLAMATION   ADVERB

as he jumped into his convertible _____ and
                                         NOUN

drove off with his _____ wife.
                        ADJECTIVE

"_____OUCH_____!" he said _____HAPPILY_____
  EXCLAMATION   ADVERB

as he jumped into his convertible _____CAT_____ and
                                         NOUN

drove off with his _____BRAVE_____ wife.
                        ADJECTIVE

MAD LIBS®

QUICK REVIEW

In case you have forgotten what adjectives, adverbs, nouns, and verbs are, here is a quick review:

An ADJECTIVE describes something or somebody. *Lumpy, soft, ugly, messy,* and *short* are adjectives.

An ADVERB tells how something is done. It modifies a verb and usually ends in "ly." *Modestly, stupidly, greedily,* and *carefully* are adverbs.

A NOUN is the name of a person, place, or thing. *Sidewalk, umbrella, bridle, bathtub,* and *nose* are nouns.

A VERB is an action word. *Run, pitch, jump,* and *swim* are verbs. Put the verbs in past tense if the directions say PAST TENSE. *Ran, pitched, jumped,* and *swam* are verbs in the past tense.

When we ask for A PLACE, we mean any sort of place: a country or city (*Spain, Cleveland*) or a room (*bathroom, kitchen*).

An EXCLAMATION or SILLY WORD is any sort of funny sound, gasp, grunt, or outcry, like *Wow!, Ouch!, Whomp!, Ick!,* and *Gadzooks!*

When we ask for specific words, like a NUMBER, a COLOR, an ANIMAL, or a PART OF THE BODY, we mean a word that is one of those things, like *seven, blue, horse,* or *head.*

When we ask for a PLURAL, it means more than one. For example, *cat* pluralized is *cats.*

MAD LIBS® is fun to play with friends, but you can also play it by yourself! To begin with, DO NOT look at the story on the page below. Fill in the blanks on this page with the words called for. Then, using the words you have selected, fill in the blank spaces in the story.

Now you've created your own hilarious MAD LIBS® game!

FAMOUS CATS

ADJECTIVE _____

NOUN _____

NUMBER _____

TYPE OF FOOD _____

PLURAL NOUN _____

VERB _____

PERSON IN ROOM _____

CELEBRITY _____

PLURAL NOUN _____

NOUN _____

PART OF THE BODY _____

A PLACE _____

FIRST NAME _____

ADJECTIVE _____

ANIMAL _____

MAD LIBS
FAMOUS CATS

From cartoons to social media, cats are everywhere. Here are a few of the most famous cats:

- Morris—the cat with the _____ attitude and the posh
  <u>ADJECTIVE</u>

  _____ is the "spokesperson" for _____ Lives cat
  <u>NOUN</u>   <u>NUMBER</u>

  _____.
  <u>TYPE OF FOOD</u>

- Garfield—the famous comic-strip cat who hates _____, loves
  <u>PLURAL NOUN</u>

  to _____, and has no respect for _____, his
     <u>VERB</u>   <u>PERSON IN ROOM</u>

  owner's dog.

- Smelly Cat—made famous in the song sung by _____ on the
  <u>CELEBRITY</u>

  TV show _____.
          <u>PLURAL NOUN</u>

- Grumpy Cat—an Internet _____ known for her hilarious
                          <u>NOUN</u>

  _____ expressions.
  <u>PART OF THE BODY</u>

- Stubbs—the mayor of (the) _____, Alaska.
                            <u>A PLACE</u>

- Cat—the feline heroine of the movie *Breakfast at* _____'s.
                                                      <u>FIRST NAME</u>

- Tom—the _____ cat that will never catch his archenemy,
         <u>ADJECTIVE</u>

  Jerry the _____.
            <u>ANIMAL</u>

MAD LIBS® is fun to play with friends, but you can also play it by yourself! To begin with, DO NOT look at the story on the page below. Fill in the blanks on this page with the words called for. Then, using the words you have selected, fill in the blank spaces in the story.

Now you've created your own hilarious MAD LIBS® game!

WHICH BREED IS RIGHT FOR YOU?

PART OF THE BODY (PLURAL) _____

ADJECTIVE _____

NOUN _____

ADJECTIVE _____

NOUN _____

NOUN _____

PART OF THE BODY (PLURAL) _____

ADJECTIVE _____

NOUN _____

SILLY WORD _____

ADJECTIVE _____

A PLACE _____

ADJECTIVE _____

PART OF THE BODY _____

COLOR _____

ADJECTIVE _____

NOUN _____

MAD LIBS®
WHICH BREED IS RIGHT FOR YOU?

So you're thinking of getting a cat. Whether you prefer cats with no

_____ or _____ ears, there's a/an _____
PART OF THE BODY (PLURAL)   ADJECTIVE   NOUN

for you.

Sphynx: If you go for the _____ things in life, and don't want to
                                    ADJECTIVE

have to clean up cat hair, this is the _____ for you.
                                            NOUN

Siamese: Do you want a cat that sounds like a crying _____ and has
                                                              NOUN

crossed _____? Well then, go get a Siamese.
        PART OF THE BODY (PLURAL)

Manx: Looking for a cat with a sweet, _____ face and no
                                               ADJECTIVE

_____? We suggest you get a/an _____.
    NOUN   SILLY WORD

Maine coon: How about a cat that's the size of a/an _____ dog? If
                                                              ADJECTIVE

you don't mind having to brush your cat every day, it sounds like you should

get a/an _____ coon.
            A PLACE

Persian: If you love a/an _____-looking cat with a scrunched-up
                                    ADJECTIVE

_____, go get yourself a Persian.
PART OF THE BODY

Snowshoe: Do you love a cat with adorable _____ feet and a/an
                                                    COLOR

_____ personality? You may want a/an _____-shoe.
    ADJECTIVE   NOUN

MAD LIBS® is fun to play with friends, but you can also play it by yourself! To begin with, DO NOT look at the story on the page below. Fill in the blanks on this page with the words called for. Then, using the words you have selected, fill in the blank spaces in the story.

Now you've created your own hilarious MAD LIBS® game!

CAT SAYINGS

ADJECTIVE _____

PLURAL NOUN _____

PART OF THE BODY _____

NOUN _____

SILLY WORD _____

ADJECTIVE _____

VERB ENDING IN "ING" _____

ARTICLE OF CLOTHING _____

ADJECTIVE _____

NOUN _____

ANIMAL _____

NOUN _____

NOUN _____

EXCLAMATION _____

ADJECTIVE _____

ADVERB _____

ADJECTIVE _____

MAD●LIBS®
CAT SAYINGS

There are a lot of _____ phrases that incorporate our favorite feline
                          ADJECTIVE

_____. Check out these sayings and their meanings:
   PLURAL NOUN

- Cat got your _____?: Why aren't you talking?
                 PART OF THE BODY

- You let the cat out of the _____: _____! My secret
                              NOUN   SILLY WORD

isn't so _____ anymore.
          ADJECTIVE

- It is raining cats and dogs: It is _____ like crazy.
                                     VERB ENDING IN "ING"

- That is the cat's _____: That is totally _____!
                     ARTICLE OF CLOTHING   ADJECTIVE

- When the cat's away, the mice will play: The boss is away—let's get this

_____ started!
   NOUN

- Curiosity killed the _____: Mind your own _____!
                        ANIMAL   NOUN

- He is a fat cat: He likes to flash his _____.
                                          NOUN

- Looks like something the cat dragged in: _____! You look
                                            EXCLAMATION

_____. What happened?!
   ADJECTIVE

- Cat on a hot tin roof: Please sit _____!
                                     ADVERB

- It's like herding cats: This job is totally _____!
                                               ADJECTIVE

MAD LIBS® is fun to play with friends, but you can also play it by yourself! To begin with, DO NOT look at the story on the page below. Fill in the blanks on this page with the words called for. Then, using the words you have selected, fill in the blank spaces in the story.

Now you've created your own hilarious MAD LIBS® game!

CAT SHOWS

ADJECTIVE _____

ADJECTIVE _____

ADJECTIVE _____

VERB _____

NOUN _____

SAME NOUN _____

NOUN _____

NOUN _____

PLURAL NOUN _____

PLURAL NOUN _____

NOUN _____

A PLACE _____

PLURAL NOUN _____

ADJECTIVE _____

NOUN _____

MAD LIBS
CAT SHOWS

There are some cat owners who take their love of cats to a/an _____
ADJECTIVE

level. A/An _____ example of this: the cat show. Both _____
ADJECTIVE   ADJECTIVE

and purebred cats are allowed to _____ in a cat show, although the
VERB

rules differ from _____ to _____. The cats are compared
NOUN   SAME NOUN

to a breed _____, and those judged to be closest to it are awarded
NOUN

a/an _____. At the end of the year, all the _____ who
NOUN   PLURAL NOUN

won at various shows are tallied up, and regional and national _____
PLURAL NOUN

are presented. The very first cat _____ took place in 1598 at (the)
NOUN

_____ in England. In the United States, the first cat shows were held
A PLACE

at New England country _____ in the 1860s. The most important
PLURAL NOUN

cat show in the United States is the CFA _____ Cat Show. But no
ADJECTIVE

matter which cat wins "Best in Show," every cat is a/an _____—to
NOUN

their owners, at least!

MAD LIBS® is fun to play with friends, but you can also play it by yourself! To begin with, DO NOT look at the story on the page below. Fill in the blanks on this page with the words called for. Then, using the words you have selected, fill in the blank spaces in the story.

Now you've created your own hilarious MAD LIBS® game!

CATS IN THE NEWS

PLURAL NOUN _____

ADJECTIVE _____

NOUN _____

ADJECTIVE _____

NUMBER _____

NOUN _____

NOUN _____

NOUN _____

SAME NOUN _____

ADJECTIVE _____

NOUN _____

ADJECTIVE _____

NOUN _____

VERB _____

MAD LIBS
CATS IN THE NEWS

News Anchor #1: Stay tuned, _____! After the commercial break, we

PLURAL NOUN

have a/an _____ story about a cat who saved a young _____

ADJECTIVE   NOUN

from a/an _____ dog.

ADJECTIVE

News Anchor #2: That reminds me of the story about the cat that dialed

_____-1-1 after its owner fell out of his _____.

NUMBER   NOUN

News Anchor #1: And how about that kitten that survived the deadly

_____ in Taiwan?

NOUN

News Anchor #2: Have you heard about the kitten that was saved from a/an

_____ by a/an _____-fighter with _____ water

NOUN   SAME NOUN   ADJECTIVE

and a/an _____ full of oxygen?

NOUN

News Anchor #1: And who could forget that _____ story about a

ADJECTIVE

cat that took a/an _____ on the London Underground?

NOUN

News Anchor #2: Well, I guess he had to _____ to work just like

VERB

everyone else!

MAD LIBS® is fun to play with friends, but you can also play it by yourself! To begin with, DO NOT look at the story on the page below. Fill in the blanks on this page with the words called for. Then, using the words you have selected, fill in the blank spaces in the story.

Now you've created your own hilarious MAD LIBS® game!

HISTORY OF CATS

VERB ENDING IN "ING" _____

NUMBER _____

ADJECTIVE _____

ANIMAL (PLURAL) _____

SAME ANIMAL (PLURAL) _____

ADJECTIVE _____

PLURAL NOUN _____

ADJECTIVE _____

PART OF THE BODY _____

ADJECTIVE _____

OCCUPATION (PLURAL) _____

VERB (PAST TENSE) _____

ADJECTIVE _____

ADJECTIVE _____

NUMBER _____

ADJECTIVE _____

MAD LIBS
HISTORY OF CATS

Cats have been _____ with—or at least tolerating—people for
      VERB ENDING IN "ING"

over _____ years. Cats first became a part of our _____ lives
    NUMBER   ADJECTIVE

when people started to grow grain. The grain attracted _____,
         ANIMAL (PLURAL)

and the cats preyed on the _____. Cats soon became
        SAME ANIMAL (PLURAL)

a/an _____ fixture in people's _____ and were even
    ADJECTIVE   PLURAL NOUN

worshipped in _____ Egypt. There was even an Egyptian goddess
     ADJECTIVE

who had the _____ of a cat! However, in the _____
    PART OF THE BODY   ADJECTIVE

Ages, cats came to be demonized and were thought to be affiliated with evil

_____. Many cats were _____ to ward off evil. In
  OCCUPATION (PLURAL)   VERB (PAST TENSE)

the 1600s, the cat's _____ reputation was restored, and today cats
       ADJECTIVE

are _____ stars and live in _____ percent of American
   ADJECTIVE   NUMBER

households. Talk about a long and _____ history!
        ADJECTIVE

MAD LIBS® is fun to play with friends, but you can also play it by yourself! To begin with, DO NOT look at the story on the page below. Fill in the blanks on this page with the words called for. Then, using the words you have selected, fill in the blank spaces in the story.

Now you've created your own hilarious MAD LIBS® game!

I AM A CAT LADY

ADJECTIVE _____

ADJECTIVE _____

PLURAL NOUN _____

NUMBER _____

ADJECTIVE _____

ADJECTIVE _____

VERB _____

ADJECTIVE _____

PLURAL NOUN _____

ADVERB _____

ADVERB _____

NOUN _____

ADJECTIVE _____

ADJECTIVE _____

ADJECTIVE _____

ANIMAL _____

MAD LIBS
I AM A CAT LADY

Dear _____ Neighbor,
    ADJECTIVE

I'm glad we have come to a/an _____ understanding about our
                                       ADJECTIVE

_____. You have come to accept my _____ cats, and
PLURAL NOUN   NUMBER

I have come to accept your _____ dog. Yes, my _____
                        ADJECTIVE   ADJECTIVE

cats may _____ in your garden, but your _____ dog
         VERB   ADJECTIVE

digs up my _____. And I will remind you that my cats purr very
     PLURAL NOUN

_____, while your dog barks _____. To conclude, I feel
  ADVERB   ADVERB

sorry for the _____-man, who is scared of your _____
         NOUN   ADJECTIVE

dog, while he brings treats for my _____ felines. I'm glad we have
                         ADJECTIVE

been able to come to a/an _____ understanding on this matter.
                 ADJECTIVE

Yours truly,

The _____ Lady Next Door
    ANIMAL

MAD LIBS® is fun to play with friends, but you can also play it by yourself! To begin with, DO NOT look at the story on the page below. Fill in the blanks on this page with the words called for. Then, using the words you have selected, fill in the blank spaces in the story.

Now you've created your own hilarious MAD LIBS® game!

CATS ON CAMERA

ADJECTIVE _____

VERB ENDING IN "ING" _____

NOUN _____

SILLY WORD _____

ADJECTIVE _____

ADJECTIVE _____

NOUN _____

NOUN _____

NOUN _____

EXCLAMATION _____

VERB ENDING IN "S" _____

NOUN _____

ADJECTIVE _____

NUMBER _____

ADJECTIVE _____

PLURAL NOUN _____

MAD LIBS
CATS ON CAMERA

Cat Lover #1: Have you seen the _____ video on YouTube of the cat
<u>ADJECTIVE</u>

_____ a/an _____?
<u>VERB ENDING IN "ING"</u>   <u>NOUN</u>

Cat Lover #2: _____! It's almost as _____ as that GIF of
<u>SILLY WORD</u>   <u>ADJECTIVE</u>

the _____ kitten playing with a/an _____.
<u>ADJECTIVE</u>   <u>NOUN</u>

Cat Lover #1: And that clip of the _____ cat who pushes her own
<u>NOUN</u>

_____ down some stairs?! _____!
<u>NOUN</u>   <u>EXCLAMATION</u>

Cat Lover #2: How about the cat who _____ along to
<u>VERB ENDING IN "S"</u>

a/an _____ video? Totally _____!
<u>NOUN</u>   <u>ADJECTIVE</u>

Cat Lover #1: And there must be about _____ videos of
<u>NUMBER</u>

_____ cats that have gotten stuck in _____.
<u>ADJECTIVE</u>   <u>PLURAL NOUN</u>

Cat Lover #2: Yep! And I think I've watched them all.

MAD LIBS® is fun to play with friends, but you can also play it by yourself! To begin with, DO NOT look at the story on the page below. Fill in the blanks on this page with the words called for. Then, using the words you have selected, fill in the blank spaces in the story.

Now you've created your own hilarious MAD LIBS® game!

SEVEN SIGNS YOUR CAT LOVES YOU

ADJECTIVE _____

NOUN _____

SAME NOUN _____

PLURAL NOUN _____

ADJECTIVE _____

VERB _____

NOUN _____

SAME NOUN _____

ADVERB _____

NOUN _____

ADJECTIVE _____

ANIMAL _____

A PLACE _____

ADJECTIVE _____

Here are seven _____ signs your cat loves you:
ADJECTIVE

• Head butting—If your boyfriend or _____ did this to you,
NOUN

you probably wouldn't want them as your _____ anymore.
SAME NOUN

But when your cat does it, they are marking you with their facial

_____, which shows your cat trusts you.
PLURAL NOUN

• Powerful purrs—Cats purr for all kinds of reasons, but that

_____ body rumble is saved for expressing true love.
ADJECTIVE

• Love bites—If your cat likes to _____ on you, it means they
VERB

have a serious _____ for you.
NOUN

• Tail twitching—When the tip of a cat's _____ is twitching, it
SAME NOUN

means they are in total control.

• Tummy up—If your cat rolls around on the ground with its tummy

showing, it means they trust you _____.
ADVERB

• Kneading—No, your cat doesn't think you are _____ dough;
NOUN

he is reliving his _____ memories of kittenhood.
ADJECTIVE

• Gifts—You may not want to find a dead _____ in your
ANIMAL

_____, but this is a/an _____ sign of friendship.
A PLACE   ADJECTIVE

MAD LIBS® is fun to play with friends, but you can also play it by yourself! To begin with, DO NOT look at the story on the page below. Fill in the blanks on this page with the words called for. Then, using the words you have selected, fill in the blank spaces in the story.

Now you've created your own hilarious MAD LIBS® game!

SEVEN SIGNS YOUR CAT IS TRYING TO KILL YOU

ADJECTIVE _____

PLURAL NOUN _____

ADVERB _____

NOUN _____

PART OF THE BODY _____

VERB ENDING IN "ING" _____

ADJECTIVE _____

PART OF THE BODY _____

SILLY WORD _____

NOUN _____

ADVERB _____

ANIMAL _____

ADJECTIVE _____

MAD LIBS®
SEVEN SIGNS YOUR CAT IS TRYING TO KILL YOU

There's a flip side to all those _____ expressions of love.
<u>ADJECTIVE</u>

- Head butting—Beware! Your cat is not showing you that it trusts you; it's telling you that your _____ are numbered!
<u>PLURAL NOUN</u>

- Powerful purrs—This is not a sign of true love; it's _____ a
<u>ADVERB</u>
battle cry!

- Love bites—Not actually a/an _____ of love, but your cat
<u>NOUN</u>
tasting you to decide which bit of you to eat first. _____,
<u>PART OF THE BODY</u>
please!

- Tail twitching—The equivalent of your cat _____ a sword
<u>VERB ENDING IN "ING"</u>
at you.

- Tummy up—Do not fall for this _____ trick! As soon as
<u>ADJECTIVE</u>
you put your _____ near your cat's belly, it will scratch the
<u>PART OF THE BODY</u>
_____ out of it!
<u>SILLY WORD</u>

- Kneading—This is not a/an _____ of affection; your cat is
<u>NOUN</u>
_____ checking your organs for weaknesses.
<u>ADVERB</u>

- Gifts—A dead _____ is not a gift; it's a/an _____
<u>ANIMAL</u>   <u>ADJECTIVE</u>
warning. Didn't you see *The Godfather*?!

From MEOW LIBS® • Copyright © 2015 by Penguin Random House LLC

MAD LIBS® is fun to play with friends, but you can also play it by yourself! To begin with, DO NOT look at the story on the page below. Fill in the blanks on this page with the words called for. Then, using the words you have selected, fill in the blank spaces in the story.

Now you've created your own hilarious MAD LIBS® game!

DOGS VERSUS CATS

ADJECTIVE _____

NOUN _____

ADJECTIVE _____

ADJECTIVE _____

ADJECTIVE _____

PART OF THE BODY (PLURAL) _____

NOUN _____

VERB ENDING IN "ING" _____

NOUN _____

ANIMAL _____

NOUN _____

NOUN _____

ADJECTIVE _____

ADVERB _____

ADJECTIVE _____

MAD LIBS
DOGS VERSUS CATS

If you've ever owned both dogs and cats, you know that the differences between

the two species are _____. They are like night and _____.
　　　　　　　　　　　　　　ADJECTIVE　　　　　　　　　　　　　　　　　　　NOUN

The argument about which pet is more _____ will continue
　　　　　　　　　　　　　　　　　　　　ADJECTIVE

until the end of time, but it's easy to see why cats are _____.
　　　　　　　　　　　　　　　　　　　　　　　　　　　　　ADJECTIVE

For instance, cats won't embarrass you in front of your guests by parading

around with your _____ underwear in their _____.
　　　　　　　　　ADJECTIVE　　　　　　　　　　　　　PART OF THE BODY (PLURAL)

Cats are also funnier than dogs, even if they don't know it. And they don't

give a/an _____ if you laugh at them, because they are too busy
　　　　　　NOUN

_____ their revenge. Cats are natural _____
VERB ENDING IN "ING"　　　　　　　　　　　　　　　　　　　　NOUN

repellents—no spider, fly, or _____ stands a chance if there's
　　　　　　　　　　　　　　　ANIMAL

a cat in the _____. Cats have no interest in being hooked up to
　　　　　　　NOUN

a/an _____ and going for a walk; they'd rather curl up and take
　　　NOUN

a/an _____ nap. And it's _____ proven that cat owners are
　　　ADJECTIVE　　　　　　　　　　ADVERB

smarter and more _____ than dog owners. So go get yourself a cat!
　　　　　　　　　ADJECTIVE

MAD LIBS® is fun to play with friends, but you can also play it by yourself! To begin with, DO NOT look at the story on the page below. Fill in the blanks on this page with the words called for. Then, using the words you have selected, fill in the blank spaces in the story.

Now you've created your own hilarious MAD LIBS® game!

MY HOUSE. MY RULES.

ADJECTIVE _____

NOUN _____

VERB _____

NOUN _____

SAME NOUN _____

TYPE OF LIQUID _____

VERB ENDING IN "ING" _____

PERSON IN ROOM _____

VERB _____

SAME VERB _____

ADJECTIVE _____

ADJECTIVE _____

_____ Servant,
ADJECTIVE

It's quite obvious that you think you control me, but we all know that I am

in charge of this _____. You think I am just a simple cat, but I am
NOUN

able to out-_____ you any day of the week. Please be aware that
VERB

"your" house is actually mine, and I am not to be disturbed if I happen to

be sleeping on your bed or favorite piece of _____. I will scratch
NOUN

any piece of _____ I want. I do not want to drink _____
SAME NOUN   TYPE OF LIQUID

from an ordinary bowl; I prefer to lap water from a/an _____
VERB ENDING IN "ING"

faucet or a toilet. So please remember to leave the toilet seat up—I don't care

what _____ has to say about that. Don't try to get me to
PERSON IN ROOM

_____ during the day; you should know better than that. I prefer to
VERB

_____ at night when you are asleep; this is much more fun. You are
SAME VERB

a/an _____ human, but you are my human.
ADJECTIVE

With tolerance,

Your Super-_____ Cat
ADJECTIVE

MAD LIBS® is fun to play with friends, but you can also play it by yourself! To begin with, DO NOT look at the story on the page below. Fill in the blanks on this page with the words called for. Then, using the words you have selected, fill in the blank spaces in the story.

Now you've created your own hilarious MAD LIBS® game!

AM I IN YOUR WAY?

EXCLAMATION _____

NOUN _____

NOUN _____

ADJECTIVE _____

NOUN _____

ADJECTIVE _____

VERB ENDING IN "ING" _____

NOUN _____

VERB ENDING IN "ING" _____

NOUN _____

NOUN _____

VERB _____

NOUN _____

TYPE OF FOOD _____

PART OF THE BODY _____

MAD LIBS

AM I IN YOUR WAY?

_____! Were you trying to type? I just felt the need to lie on your
   EXCLAMATION

_____ keyboard at this moment. That _____ you're trying
   NOUN   NOUN

to write isn't as _____ as my nap. Oh, and did you want to read
               ADJECTIVE

today's _____? Tough. It's much more _____ that I use
     NOUN   ADJECTIVE

it as a place to do my _____. And I hope you aren't going to
                    VERB ENDING IN "ING"

do the _____ today, as I am planning on _____ in
      NOUN   VERB ENDING IN "ING"

the laundry _____ all day, and I don't want to be disturbed. Let me
         NOUN

know when you are going to start preparing dinner, as I can help knock things

off the _____. And when you sit down to _____, I will
      NOUN   VERB

certainly expect a few pieces of food from your _____. But please,
                                   NOUN

no _____—you know I turn my _____ up at that.
  TYPE OF FOOD   PART OF THE BODY

MAD LIBS® is fun to play with friends, but you can also play it by yourself! To begin with, DO NOT look at the story on the page below. Fill in the blanks on this page with the words called for. Then, using the words you have selected, fill in the blank spaces in the story.

Now you've created your own hilarious MAD LIBS® game!

THE SEVEN HABITS OF HIGHLY EFFECTIVE KITTENS

PLURAL NOUN _____

ADJECTIVE _____

NOUN _____

VERB ENDING IN "ING" _____

PART OF THE BODY _____

ADJECTIVE _____

VERB _____

ADJECTIVE _____

ANIMAL _____

NOUN _____

ADJECTIVE _____

ANIMAL _____

NOUN _____

NOUN _____

NOUN _____

NOUN _____

VERB _____

MAD LIBS®
THE SEVEN HABITS OF
HIGHLY EFFECTIVE KITTENS

All kittens know they must perfect these _____:
                                         PLURAL NOUN

1. Be as adorably _____ as possible at all times.
                   ADJECTIVE

2. Perfect that tiny, irresistible _____. Your servants will come
                                   NOUN

_____ in a/an _____-beat.
VERB ENDING IN "ING"   PART OF THE BODY

3. Learn the ways of a/an _____ ninja; you can _____
                          ADJECTIVE   VERB

anywhere. It's all about stealth.

4. You must be _____, whether you're facing down the neighbor's
               ADJECTIVE

_____ or jumping off the kitchen _____.
   ANIMAL   NOUN

5. You may be _____, but inside of you beats the heart of
              ADJECTIVE

a/an _____. Honor your heritage.
     ANIMAL

6. Make use of those _____-sharp claws. Climb the living room
                     NOUN

_____ and the Christmas _____ with courage and
   NOUN   NOUN

confidence.

7. And when you sleep, curl up in the tiniest, fluffiest _____ possible.
                                                         NOUN

It will make your servants _____.
                           VERB

MAD LIBS® is fun to play with friends, but you can also play it by yourself! To begin with, DO NOT look at the story on the page below. Fill in the blanks on this page with the words called for. Then, using the words you have selected, fill in the blank spaces in the story.

Now you've created your own hilarious MAD LIBS® game!

YOU CALL THAT CAT FOOD?

EXCLAMATION _____

NOUN _____

ADJECTIVE _____

ANIMAL _____

ADJECTIVE _____

NOUN _____

ADJECTIVE _____

NOUN _____

ADJECTIVE _____

ADJECTIVE _____

NOUN _____

PLURAL NOUN _____

ADJECTIVE _____

NOUN _____

MAD LIBS
YOU CALL THAT CAT FOOD?

_____! What is this _____ that you put in my bowl? Do
　　EXCLAMATION　　　　　　　　　　NOUN

you really expect me to eat this? Have I not made it perfectly _____
　　　　　　　　　　　　　　　　　　　　　　　　　　　　　ADJECTIVE

that I prefer fresh _____ to the _____ stuff that comes
　　　　　　　　　ANIMAL　　　　　　　ADJECTIVE

out of a/an _____? It looks _____ and smells like a rotting
　　　　　　NOUN　　　　　　　　ADJECTIVE

_____. And I refuse to eat something that is advertised by a cat who is
　NOUN

an embarrassment to my _____ species. Don't get so _____
　　　　　　　　　　　ADJECTIVE　　　　　　　　　　　　ADJECTIVE

when I jump onto the kitchen _____ to see what you are cooking for
　　　　　　　　　　　　　　NOUN

yourself—I might not want any of that, either. Some of the _____
　　　　　　　　　　　　　　　　　　　　　　　　　　PLURAL NOUN

you make look and smell as _____ as that _____ you try
　　　　　　　　　　　ADJECTIVE　　　　　　　　NOUN

to feed me!

MAD LIBS® is fun to play with friends, but you can also play it by yourself! To begin with, DO NOT look at the story on the page below. Fill in the blanks on this page with the words called for. Then, using the words you have selected, fill in the blank spaces in the story.

Now you've created your own hilarious MAD LIBS® game!

STRANGE CAT FACTS

VERB ENDING IN "ING" _____

NOUN _____

NUMBER _____

PLURAL NOUN _____

VERB _____

PLURAL NOUN _____

NUMBER _____

NUMBER _____

NOUN _____

NOUN _____

VERB _____

PART OF THE BODY _____

COLOR _____

ADJECTIVE _____

MAD LIBS
STRANGE CAT FACTS

If you think you know cats, think again:

- On average, cats spend two-thirds of every day _____.
  <u>VERB ENDING IN "ING"</u>

- A group of cats is called a/an "_____."
  <u>NOUN</u>

- A cat can jump up to _____ times its own height in a single
  <u>NUMBER</u>
bound.

- Cats have over twenty _____ that control their ears.
  <u>PLURAL NOUN</u>

- Cats can't _____ sweetness.
  <u>VERB</u>

- The world's longest cat measured 48.5 _____ long.
  <u>PLURAL NOUN</u>

- A cat has _____ toes on its front paws, but only _____
  <u>NUMBER</u>   <u>NUMBER</u>
toes on its back paws.

- When a cat leaves its _____ uncovered in the litter box, it is
  <u>NOUN</u>
a/an _____ of aggression.
  <u>NOUN</u>

- Cats only _____ through their _____ pads.
  <u>VERB</u>   <u>PART OF THE BODY</u>

- _____ cats are bad luck in the United States, but they are
  <u>COLOR</u>
_____ luck in the United Kingdom and Australia.
  <u>ADJECTIVE</u>

MAD LIBS® is fun to play with friends, but you can also play it by yourself! To begin with, DO NOT look at the story on the page below. Fill in the blanks on this page with the words called for. Then, using the words you have selected, fill in the blank spaces in the story.

Now you've created your own hilarious MAD LIBS® game!

CATS IN A BOX—OR BAG

ADJECTIVE _____

VERB _____

ANIMAL (PLURAL) _____

PLURAL NOUN _____

ADJECTIVE _____

ADJECTIVE _____

ARTICLE OF CLOTHING _____

PLURAL NOUN _____

VERB _____

SAME VERB _____

ADJECTIVE _____

NOUN _____

PLURAL NOUN _____

ADJECTIVE _____

ANIMAL (PLURAL) _____

VERB _____

MAD LIBS

CATS IN A BOX—OR BAG

Don't bother buying me some _____ toy; I won't _____ with it. So
                                   ADJECTIVE   VERB

skip the fake _____ filled with catnip and those "teasers" with
              ANIMAL (PLURAL)

_____ on the ends. Just give me an old _____ box. The secret
PLURAL NOUN   ADJECTIVE

of the old _____ box is that it gives me (a/an) _____
           ADJECTIVE   ARTICLE OF CLOTHING

of invisibility, enhancing my super-_____. When I am in the box,
                                    PLURAL NOUN

I can _____ you, but you can't _____ me. If the box is
      VERB   SAME VERB

_____, that's even better, as it is more fun if I can barely get myself in
ADJECTIVE

it. And it is preferable if the box has a/an _____ or _____.
                                             NOUN   PLURAL NOUN

And if you don't have a box, a/an _____ paper bag will do. Because
                                  ADJECTIVE

within the bag live the Bag _____. And it is my mission in life
                            ANIMAL (PLURAL)

to _____ them!
   VERB

MAD LIBS® is fun to play with friends, but you can also play it by yourself! To begin with, DO NOT look at the story on the page below. Fill in the blanks on this page with the words called for. Then, using the words you have selected, fill in the blank spaces in the story.

Now you've created your own hilarious MAD LIBS® game!

BIG CATS

VERB _____

PLURAL NOUN _____

PLURAL NOUN _____

ADJECTIVE _____

ADJECTIVE _____

ANIMAL _____

SAME ANIMAL _____

ADJECTIVE _____

ADJECTIVE _____

VERB _____

SAME VERB _____

ADJECTIVE _____

VERB ENDING IN "ING" _____

SAME VERB ENDING IN "ING" _____

A PLACE _____

ADJECTIVE _____

NOUN _____

ADJECTIVE _____

MAD LIBS
BIG CATS

Although they don't have to _____ for their food or worry about
                              VERB

_____, domestic cats aren't all that different from their wild
  PLURAL NOUN

_____ and sisters. All cats, domestic and _____, are
  PLURAL NOUN   ADJECTIVE

_____ carnivores, whether they prefer to eat a can of _____
  ADJECTIVE   ANIMAL

delight or an entire raw _____. Felines around the world, from
                              SAME ANIMAL

_____ tabbies to _____ jaguars, _____ for sixteen to
  ADJECTIVE   ADJECTIVE   VERB

twenty hours a day. (However, snow leopards don't get to _____
                                                            SAME VERB

in a basket of _____ laundry.) And there's the _____
                  ADJECTIVE   VERB ENDING IN "ING"

thing. You might think your cat is _____ against you
                                      SAME VERB ENDING IN "ING"

because it loves you. But it's marking you, just like big cats mark their territory

in (the) _____. And even though there are _____
            A PLACE   ADJECTIVE

similarities between a house cat and a cheetah, it's much safer to have a domestic

cat in your _____—so don't get any _____ ideas!
               NOUN   ADJECTIVE

MAD LIBS® is fun to play with friends, but you can also play it by yourself! To begin with, DO NOT look at the story on the page below. Fill in the blanks on this page with the words called for. Then, using the words you have selected, fill in the blank spaces in the story.

Now you've created your own hilarious MAD LIBS® game!

CATS IN BOOKS

ADJECTIVE _____

ADJECTIVE _____

VERB ENDING IN "ING" _____

ADJECTIVE _____

PERSON IN ROOM _____

PART OF THE BODY _____

PERSON IN ROOM _____

A PLACE _____

ADJECTIVE _____

ADJECTIVE _____

PLURAL NOUN _____

PART OF THE BODY _____

ADJECTIVE _____

PLURAL NOUN _____

ADJECTIVE _____

PART OF THE BODY _____

MAD LIBS
CATS IN BOOKS

Test your knowledge about cats who have made their _____ mark in
ADJECTIVE

literature:

- The cat who seems to be _____ and can't stop
ADJECTIVE

_____ at Alice: the Cheshire Cat
VERB ENDING IN "ING"

- The _____ cat in _____ King's horror
ADJECTIVE   PERSON IN ROOM

classic: Church

- The cat with a squashed _____ who belongs to
PART OF THE BODY

_____ Potter's best friend: Crookshanks
PERSON IN ROOM

- The _____ cat who is the best friend of the _____
A PLACE   ADJECTIVE

cockroach Archy: Mehitabel

- A mysterious, _____, and small black cat capable of
ADJECTIVE

performing _____ of magic and sleight of _____:
PLURAL NOUN   PART OF THE BODY

Mr. Mistoffelees

- The story of a very _____ kitten who struggles to keep his
ADJECTIVE

_____ clean and tidy: *Tom Kitten*
PLURAL NOUN

- A/An _____ tale about a cat who wins the _____
ADJECTIVE   PART OF THE BODY

of a princess in marriage: *Puss in Boots*

MAD LIBS® is fun to play with friends, but you can also play it by yourself! To begin with, DO NOT look at the story on the page below. Fill in the blanks on this page with the words called for. Then, using the words you have selected, fill in the blank spaces in the story.

Now you've created your own hilarious MAD LIBS® game!

DRESSING YOUR CAT

ADJECTIVE _____

NOUN _____

PART OF THE BODY (PLURAL) _____

ANIMAL _____

ADJECTIVE _____

PERSON IN ROOM (MALE) _____

COLOR _____

PLURAL NOUN _____

OCCUPATION _____

NOUN _____

NOUN _____

ARTICLE OF CLOTHING _____

ADJECTIVE _____

NOUN _____

ADVERB _____

ADJECTIVE _____

MAD☺LIBS
DRESSING YOUR CAT

Your cat can help you celebrate your favorite holidays throughout the year. All

you need to do is dress it up in a/an _____, fun _____.
                                    ADJECTIVE   NOUN

With a pair of fuzzy _____, your cat can be transformed
                    PART OF THE BODY (PLURAL)

into the Easter _____. Or be _____ and turn your
               ANIMAL   ADJECTIVE

cat into Uncle _____ with a little red, white, and
              PERSON IN ROOM (MALE)

_____ suit. And there are a lot of _____ for your cat to wear
COLOR   PLURAL NOUN

on Halloween. You can dress your cat as a/an _____ in a pink tutu,
                                             OCCUPATION

a prehistoric _____ with spikes down its back, or a superhero like
              NOUN

_____-man with a black cape and matching _____.
NOUN   ARTICLE OF CLOTHING

And of course any cat can be turned into Santa Claus with a/an _____
                                                              ADJECTIVE

red suit and a cute matching _____. Just make sure you choose
                             NOUN

_____—you don't want to get on your cat's _____ side!
ADVERB   ADJECTIVE

MAD LIBS® is fun to play with friends, but you can also play it by yourself! To begin with, DO NOT look at the story on the page below. Fill in the blanks on this page with the words called for. Then, using the words you have selected, fill in the blank spaces in the story.

Now you've created your own hilarious MAD LIBS® game!

NINE LIVES

NOUN _____

ADJECTIVE _____

VERB ENDING IN "ING" _____

ADJECTIVE _____

ADJECTIVE _____

ANIMAL _____

ADJECTIVE _____

NOUN _____

NUMBER _____

TYPE OF LIQUID _____

NOUN _____

VERB (PAST TENSE) _____

NOUN _____

ADJECTIVE _____

VEHICLE _____

NOUN _____

NOUN _____

ADJECTIVE _____

MAD LIBS

NINE LIVES

Life #1—I ate a/an _____ — a/an _____ mistake.
NOUN   ADJECTIVE

Life #2—I didn't look both ways before _____ the street.
VERB ENDING IN "ING"

_____ move.
ADJECTIVE

Life #3—I was a bit too _____ when I teased the neighbor's
ADJECTIVE

_____ .
ANIMAL

Life #4—I thought cats were supposed to be able to survive falls from

_____ places?!
ADJECTIVE

Life #5—I got locked in the _____ for _____ days without
NOUN   NUMBER

food or _____ . What's a/an _____ to do?!
TYPE OF LIQUID   NOUN

Life #6—I _____ into the washing machine. That spin cycle is a
VERB (PAST TENSE)

killer, let me tell you . . .

Life #7—I chewed through the cord to the _____ . That was
NOUN

a/an _____ shocker.
ADJECTIVE

Life #8—I was keeping warm under the _____ when my human
VEHICLE

decided to start it. I should have just taken a nap in the _____ basket.
NOUN

I have one _____ left—better make it _____ !
NOUN   ADJECTIVE

MAD LIBS®

DOG ATE MY MAD LIBS

by Leigh Olsen

MAD LIBS®

INSTRUCTIONS

MAD LIBS® is a game for people who don't like games!
It can be played by one, two, three, four, or forty.

• RIDICULOUSLY SIMPLE DIRECTIONS

In this tablet you will find stories containing blank spaces where words are left out. One player, the READER, selects one of these stories. The READER does not tell anyone what the story is about. Instead, he/she asks the other players, the WRITERS, to give him/her words. These words are used to fill in the blank spaces in the story.

• TO PLAY

The READER asks each WRITER in turn to call out a word—an adjective or a noun or whatever the space calls for—and uses them to fill in the blank spaces in the story. The result is a MAD LIBS® game.

When the READER then reads the completed MAD LIBS® game to the other players, they will discover that they have written a story that is fantastic, screamingly funny, shocking, silly, crazy, or just plain dumb—depending upon which words each WRITER called out.

• EXAMPLE (*Before* and *After*)

" _____!" he said _____
        EXCLAMATION   ADVERB

as he jumped into his convertible _____ and
                                          NOUN

drove off with his _____ wife.
                          ADJECTIVE

" _____OUCH_____!" he said _____HAPPILY_____
        EXCLAMATION   ADVERB

as he jumped into his convertible _____CAT_____ and
                                          NOUN

drove off with his _____BRAVE_____ wife.
                          ADJECTIVE

MAD LIBS®

QUICK REVIEW

In case you have forgotten what adjectives, adverbs, nouns, and verbs are, here is a quick review:

An ADJECTIVE describes something or somebody. *Lumpy, soft, ugly, messy,* and *short* are adjectives.

An ADVERB tells how something is done. It modifies a verb and usually ends in "ly." *Modestly, stupidly, greedily,* and *carefully* are adverbs.

A NOUN is the name of a person, place, or thing. *Sidewalk, umbrella, bridle, bathtub,* and *nose* are nouns.

A VERB is an action word. *Run, pitch, jump,* and *swim* are verbs. Put the verbs in past tense if the directions say PAST TENSE. *Ran, pitched, jumped,* and *swam* are verbs in the past tense.

When we ask for A PLACE, we mean any sort of place: a country or city *(Spain, Cleveland)* or a room *(bathroom, kitchen).*

An EXCLAMATION or SILLY WORD is any sort of funny sound, gasp, grunt, or outcry, like *Wow!, Ouch!, Whomp!, Ick!,* and *Gadzooks!*

When we ask for specific words, like a NUMBER, a COLOR, an ANIMAL, or a PART OF THE BODY, we mean a word that is one of those things, like *seven, blue, horse,* or *head.*

When we ask for a PLURAL, it means more than one. For example, *cat* pluralized is *cats.*

MAD LIBS® is fun to play with friends, but you can also play it by yourself! To begin with, DO NOT look at the story on the page below. Fill in the blanks on this page with the words called for. Then, using the words you have selected, fill in the blank spaces in the story.

Now you've created your own hilarious MAD LIBS® game!

DOG DAYS

VERB ENDING IN "ING" _____

PART OF THE BODY _____

PLURAL NOUN _____

VERB _____

NOUN _____

A PLACE _____

ADVERB _____

NOUN _____

PLURAL NOUN _____

PART OF THE BODY _____

PART OF THE BODY _____

PLURAL NOUN _____

PLURAL NOUN _____

NOUN _____

MAD LIBS

DOG DAYS

Have you always wondered what it's like to be a dog?

7:00 a.m.: I wake up and my tummy is _____. I bug my human
                                        VERB ENDING IN "ING"

by licking her _____ until I get a bowl of _____.
                PART OF THE BODY   PLURAL NOUN

7:30 a.m.: Potty time! My human takes me outside to _____ on a/an
                                                     VERB

_____.
   NOUN

8:00 a.m.: My human leaves to go to (the) _____. I am sad and pout
                                           A PLACE

_____.
   ADVERB

9:00 a.m.: Nap time. I cuddle on my favorite _____ and dream about
                                              NOUN

chasing _____.
         PLURAL NOUN

6:00 p.m.: MY HUMAN IS HOME! FINALLY! I wag my _____
                                                PART OF THE BODY

back and forth, and give my human kisses on the _____.
                                                 PART OF THE BODY

6:30 p.m.: My human takes me for a walk, and I sniff lots of _____.
                                                             PLURAL NOUN

7:00 p.m.: Dinnertime! Eating _____ is my favorite!
                               PLURAL NOUN

9:00 p.m.: I snuggle up next to my human and fall asleep, happy as

a/an _____.
      NOUN

MAD LIBS® is fun to play with friends, but you can also play it by yourself! To begin with, DO NOT look at the story on the page below. Fill in the blanks on this page with the words called for. Then, using the words you have selected, fill in the blank spaces in the story.

Now you've created your own hilarious MAD LIBS® game!

WHO'S THAT DOG?, PART 1

A PLACE _____

NOUN _____

PLURAL NOUN _____

VERB _____

VERB ENDING IN "ING" _____

ADJECTIVE _____

ADJECTIVE _____

ADJECTIVE _____

NOUN _____

ADJECTIVE _____

ADJECTIVE _____

VERB _____

A PLACE _____

NOUN _____

MAD LIBS®
WHO'S THAT DOG?, PART 1

With hundreds of breeds of dogs in (the) _____, there's one for every
         A PLACE

kind of _____. Here are a few popular breeds:
     NOUN

Golden retriever: The golden retriever is one of the most popular family

_____. Intelligent and eager to _____, the golden retriever
   PLURAL NOUN   VERB

makes an excellent _____ companion, and is also a/an
         VERB ENDING IN "ING"

_____ guide dog.
   ADJECTIVE

Pug: The pug is a lot of dog in a very _____ package. It is known
            ADJECTIVE

for being loving, outgoing, and _____. And it snores like a freight
           ADJECTIVE

_____!
   NOUN

Siberian husky: The husky was bred to pull _____ sleds, and it is
           ADJECTIVE

known for its _____ endurance and willingness to _____.
     ADJECTIVE   VERB

German shepherd: The German shepherd is not only the most popular police,

guard, and military dog in (the) _____, it is also a loving family
          A PLACE

_____.
   NOUN

MAD LIBS® is fun to play with friends, but you can also play it by yourself! To begin with, DO NOT look at the story on the page below. Fill in the blanks on this page with the words called for. Then, using the words you have selected, fill in the blank spaces in the story.

Now you've created your own hilarious MAD LIBS® game!

FAMOUS FIDOS: RIN TIN TIN

NOUN _____

PERSON IN ROOM _____

A PLACE _____

VERB _____

CELEBRITY _____

PERSON IN ROOM _____

ADJECTIVE _____

A PLACE _____

NOUN _____

NOUN _____

ADJECTIVE _____

PLURAL NOUN _____

NOUN _____

MAD LIBS®
FAMOUS FIDOS: RIN TIN TIN

Rin Tin Tin was the biggest movie-star pooch to ever grace the silver

_____. During World War I, Rin Tin Tin's owner and future
NOUN

trainer, _____, discovered the German shepherd puppy on a war-
PERSON IN ROOM

torn battlefield in (the) _____. He brought Rin Tin Tin back
A PLACE

to the United States, trained him to _____, and brought him to
VERB

Hollywood, home to celebrities like _____ and _____.
CELEBRITY   PERSON IN ROOM

Soon, Rin Tin Tin began to receive _____ roles in silent films!
ADJECTIVE

He quickly became one of the most famous stars in (the) _____.
A PLACE

In 1929, Rin Tin Tin even received the most votes for the Academy Award

for Best _____—but the Academy decided to give the award to
NOUN

a/an _____ instead. All in all, this _____ dog starred in
NOUN   ADJECTIVE

twenty-seven major motion _____. He even has his own star on the
PLURAL NOUN

Hollywood Walk of _____!
NOUN

MAD LIBS® is fun to play with friends, but you can also play it by yourself! To begin with, DO NOT look at the story on the page below. Fill in the blanks on this page with the words called for. Then, using the words you have selected, fill in the blank spaces in the story.

Now you've created your own hilarious MAD LIBS® game!

ODE TO THE MUTT

ADJECTIVE _____

PART OF THE BODY _____

PLURAL NOUN _____

PLURAL NOUN _____

PLURAL NOUN _____

NOUN _____

PART OF THE BODY _____

NOUN _____

NOUN _____

A PLACE _____

ANIMAL _____

ADJECTIVE _____

MAD LIBS®
ODE TO THE MUTT

A little bit of this and a little bit of that, the mutt is a/an _____
                                                                    ADJECTIVE

mixed-breed pup that will warm your _____ and chase your
                                      PART OF THE BODY

_____ away. First of all, mutts are just like snowflakes—no two
PLURAL NOUN

_____ are alike! Mutts come in all shapes and _____.
PLURAL NOUN   PLURAL NOUN

Big ones, small ones, fluffy ones, and scruffy ones—there's a mutt for every

_____. Mutts have a special way of worming their way into your
  NOUN

_____. There are millions in shelters that need your love and
PART OF THE BODY

_____. They need your love more than the average _____,
  NOUN   NOUN

and they'll love you to (the) _____ and back! So next time you are
                               A PLACE

thinking about bringing home a new _____, consider adopting a/an
                                      ANIMAL

_____ mutt!
  ADJECTIVE

MAD LIBS® is fun to play with friends, but you can also play it by yourself! To begin with, DO NOT look at the story on the page below. Fill in the blanks on this page with the words called for. Then, using the words you have selected, fill in the blank spaces in the story.

Now you've created your own hilarious MAD LIBS® game!

BEGGING 101

NOUN _____

ADJECTIVE _____

PLURAL NOUN _____

NOUN _____

NOUN _____

PART OF THE BODY (PLURAL) _____

ADJECTIVE _____

PART OF THE BODY (PLURAL) _____

ADVERB _____

ADJECTIVE _____

NOUN _____

TYPE OF FOOD _____

PERSON IN ROOM _____

MAD LIBS

BEGGING 101

Are your humans cooking a delicious-smelling _____? Learn to
NOUN

beg like a pro with these _____ tips, and you'll be eating tasty
ADJECTIVE

_____ in no time!
PLURAL NOUN

• Identify the weakest _____ at the dinner table. Who is the most
NOUN

likely to sneak you a/an _____? Sit as close to that person as
NOUN

possible.

• Stare up at your target with your biggest, saddest puppy-dog

_____. If possible, think of something that makes
PART OF THE BODY (PLURAL)

you feel _____ so you can work up some tears.
ADJECTIVE

• Squint your _____ so you look extra weak and
PART OF THE BODY (PLURAL)

hungry. Lie down on the ground and pout _____. Basically,
ADVERB

make yourself look as pathetic and _____ as possible.
ADJECTIVE

• Still not getting any food? Try crying like a/an _____.
NOUN

• If all else fails, grab that delicious _____ with your teeth and
TYPE OF FOOD

make a run for it—quick! Before _____ catches you!
PERSON IN ROOM

MAD LIBS® is fun to play with friends, but you can also play it by yourself! To begin with, DO NOT look at the story on the page below. Fill in the blanks on this page with the words called for. Then, using the words you have selected, fill in the blank spaces in the story.

Now you've created your own hilarious MAD LIBS® game!

DOGGY DREAMS

ADJECTIVE _____

PART OF THE BODY (PLURAL) _____

ADVERB _____

ADJECTIVE _____

EXCLAMATION _____

VERB ENDING IN "ING" _____

NOUN _____

PART OF THE BODY (PLURAL) _____

EXCLAMATION _____

NOUN _____

SAME NOUN _____

PLURAL NOUN _____

VERB _____

PART OF THE BODY (PLURAL) _____

PLURAL NOUN _____

PERSON IN ROOM _____

PART OF THE BODY _____

ADJECTIVE _____

MAD LIBS
DOGGY DREAMS

You know what it looks like when your sleeping dog is having a/an _____
ADJECTIVE

dream: Their tail swishes, their _____ twitch, and they
PART OF THE BODY (PLURAL)

bark _____. But what do dogs dream about? Here's one dog's
ADVERB

_____ dream:
ADJECTIVE

_____! What's that little flash of white fur _____
EXCLAMATION   VERB ENDING IN "ING"

in my backyard? It's a bunny _____! I have to chase it! I run, run,
NOUN

run, as fast as my _____ will carry me. Oh, _____!
PART OF THE BODY (PLURAL)   EXCLAMATION

The bunny has hidden in a/an _____! I sniff the _____,
NOUN   SAME NOUN

and sure enough, it's in there with a den of baby _____! I want
PLURAL NOUN

to play with them so bad, I could _____! I bark at the top of my
VERB

_____. Come out and play, you fluffy little _____!
PART OF THE BODY (PLURAL)   PLURAL NOUN

But before I can, _____ scratches my _____ and wakes
PERSON IN ROOM   PART OF THE BODY

me up. It was all just a/an _____ dream!
ADJECTIVE

MAD LIBS® is fun to play with friends, but you can also play it by yourself! To begin with, DO NOT look at the story on the page below. Fill in the blanks on this page with the words called for. Then, using the words you have selected, fill in the blank spaces in the story.

Now you've created your own hilarious MAD LIBS® game!

WHO'S THAT DOG?, PART 2

ADJECTIVE _____

VERB _____

ADJECTIVE _____

ADJECTIVE _____

PART OF THE BODY (PLURAL) _____

ADJECTIVE _____

ADJECTIVE _____

PLURAL NOUN _____

ADJECTIVE _____

PLURAL NOUN _____

NOUN _____

NOUN _____

More _____ dog breeds for you to love and _____!
　　　　　　ADJECTIVE　　　　　　　　　　　　　　　　　　　　VERB

Poodle: The curly-haired poodle, best known for its _____ haircut,
　　　　　　　　　　　　　　　　　　　　　　　　　　　　　ADJECTIVE

is exceptionally smart and _____.
　　　　　　　　　　　　ADJECTIVE

Dachshund: Known for its long body and short _____,
　　　　　　　　　　　　　　　　　　　　　　　PART OF THE BODY (PLURAL)

the dachshund has a friendly personality and a/an _____ sense of
　　　　　　　　　　　　　　　　　　　　　　　　ADJECTIVE

smell.

Beagle: This hunting dog is happy-go-_____, friendly, and loves
　　　　　　　　　　　　　　　　　　ADJECTIVE

the company of humans and other _____.
　　　　　　　　　　　　　　PLURAL NOUN

Great Dane: The gentle Great Dane, famous for its _____ size, is
　　　　　　　　　　　　　　　　　　　　　　　ADJECTIVE

also known as "the king of _____."
　　　　　　　　　　　PLURAL NOUN

Chihuahua: This sassy little _____, often called a "purse dog," is a
　　　　　　　　　　　　　　NOUN

big dog in a little _____.
　　　　　　　　NOUN

MAD LIBS® is fun to play with friends, but you can also play it by yourself! To begin with, DO NOT look at the story on the page below. Fill in the blanks on this page with the words called for. Then, using the words you have selected, fill in the blank spaces in the story.

Now you've created your own hilarious MAD LIBS® game!

FAMOUS FIDOS: LASSIE

ADJECTIVE _____

ADJECTIVE _____

A PLACE _____

PERSON IN ROOM (MALE) _____

ADJECTIVE _____

ADJECTIVE _____

VERB _____

ADVERB _____

PERSON IN ROOM (MALE) _____

NOUN _____

NOUN _____

NOUN _____

ADJECTIVE _____

NOUN _____

MAD LIBS®
FAMOUS FIDOS: LASSIE

Lassie the collie was famous for her heroics on television and the

_____ screen. On the TV show *Lassie*, the collie lived in
ADJECTIVE

a/an _____ farming community in (the) _____. Lassie
ADJECTIVE   A PLACE

belonged to an eleven-year-old boy named _____, as well as
PERSON IN ROOM (MALE)

his mother and _____ grandfather. Whenever the _____
ADJECTIVE   ADJECTIVE

boy got into trouble, Lassie would _____ to the rescue, or she would
VERB

run and find help. "BARK, BARK!" Lassie would say _____.
ADVERB

"What's that, girl?" the person would ask. "Little _____ fell
PERSON IN ROOM (MALE)

down a/an _____?" Quick as a/an _____, the trapped
NOUN   NOUN

_____ would be safe and _____. And once again, Lassie
NOUN   ADJECTIVE

saved the _____!
NOUN

MAD LIBS® is fun to play with friends, but you can also play it by yourself! To begin with, DO NOT look at the story on the page below. Fill in the blanks on this page with the words called for. Then, using the words you have selected, fill in the blank spaces in the story.

Now you've created your own hilarious MAD LIBS® game!

HAIL TO THE POOCH

PERSON IN ROOM _____

ADJECTIVE _____

ADJECTIVE _____

PLURAL NOUN _____

TYPE OF FOOD _____

NOUN _____

ADJECTIVE _____

ADJECTIVE _____

NOUN _____

NOUN _____

CELEBRITY _____

NOUN _____

MAD LIBS
HAIL TO THE POOCH

From George Washington to _____ to Barack Obama, many
               PERSON IN ROOM

United States presidents have been _____ dog lovers. Here's a list of
                                 ADJECTIVE

_____ First Dogs:
    ADJECTIVE

- **Laddie Boy:** Warren G. Harding once invited neighborhood

  _____ to the White House for his Airedale terrier's birthday
   PLURAL NOUN

  party, where they ate _____ made of dog biscuits!
                 TYPE OF FOOD

- **Fala:** Franklin Delano Roosevelt's beloved Scottish terrier was

  named after an Army _____ and had his own _____
                NOUN   ADJECTIVE

  secretary. Fala even starred in a/an _____ movie!
                        ADJECTIVE

- **Millie:** George H. W. Bush's springer spaniel published her own book,

  ghostwritten by the First _____, which sold more copies than
                      NOUN

  President Bush's _____!
           NOUN

- **Bo and Sunny:** Barack Obama received Bo the Portuguese water dog

  as a gift from _____. A few years later, the First Family got
          CELEBRITY

  Sunny, another Portuguese water _____.
                     NOUN

MAD LIBS® is fun to play with friends, but you can also play it by yourself! To begin with, DO NOT look at the story on the page below. Fill in the blanks on this page with the words called for. Then, using the words you have selected, fill in the blank spaces in the story.

Now you've created your own hilarious MAD LIBS® game!

CANINE CAREERS

PLURAL NOUN _____

ADJECTIVE _____

ANIMAL (PLURAL) _____

A PLACE _____

A PLACE _____

ADJECTIVE _____

PLURAL NOUN _____

PART OF THE BODY (PLURAL) _____

PLURAL NOUN _____

PLURAL NOUN _____

ADJECTIVE _____

ADJECTIVE _____

PART OF THE BODY (PLURAL) _____

PLURAL NOUN _____

MAD LIBS®
CANINE CAREERS

Not all dogs nap and play with their toy _____ all day. Some dogs
PLURAL NOUN

have _____ jobs!
ADJECTIVE

- **Guide dogs:** Guide dogs, or Seeing Eye _____, help lead
  ANIMAL (PLURAL)

  the blind where they need to go, like to (the) _____ or (the)
  A PLACE

  _____.
  A PLACE

- **Military dogs:** These dogs help troops in _____ military
  ADJECTIVE

  missions. They act as guard dogs, looking out for _____,
  PLURAL NOUN

  and they use their powerful _____ to sniff out
  PART OF THE BODY (PLURAL)

  dangerous _____. US Air Force dogs even jump out of flying
  PLURAL NOUN

  _____ with their airmen!
  PLURAL NOUN

- **Search-and-rescue dogs:** In a/an _____ disaster or
  ADJECTIVE

  in the _____ wilderness, these dogs use their powerful
  ADJECTIVE

  _____ to help track down missing _____.
  PART OF THE BODY (PLURAL) PLURAL NOUN

MAD LIBS® is fun to play with friends, but you can also play it by yourself! To begin with, DO NOT look at the story on the page below. Fill in the blanks on this page with the words called for. Then, using the words you have selected, fill in the blank spaces in the story.

Now you've created your own hilarious MAD LIBS® game!

DIVA DOG

ADJECTIVE _____

NOUN _____

PART OF THE BODY _____

SILLY WORD _____

SAME SILLY WORD _____

A PLACE _____

NOUN _____

NOUN _____

NOUN _____

PART OF THE BODY _____

ADJECTIVE _____

VERB ENDING IN "S" _____

ADJECTIVE _____

PART OF THE BODY _____

ADJECTIVE _____

NOUN _____

MAD LIBS®
DIVA DOG

Who's that _____ pooch with the fluffy little _____
        ADJECTIVE   NOUN

and the cute _____? Why, that's Little Miss _____!
           PART OF THE BODY   SILLY WORD

Little Miss _____ is famous throughout (the) _____.
          SAME SILLY WORD   A PLACE

Her _____ is splashed all over the Internet, and in books and
       NOUN

magazines like _____ *Weekly* and *Life &* _____. Little
              NOUN   NOUN

Miss can't go anywhere without someone recognizing her _____!
                                                    PART OF THE BODY

Luckily, Little Miss likes attention from the _____ pup-parazzi. She
                                            ADJECTIVE

_____ for the cameras, and greets all her _____ fans with
VERB ENDING IN "S"   ADJECTIVE

a smile on her _____. After all, without her _____ fans,
           PART OF THE BODY   ADJECTIVE

Little Miss would be just another cute face in the _____!
                                                NOUN

MAD LIBS® is fun to play with friends, but you can also play it by yourself! To begin with, DO NOT look at the story on the page below. Fill in the blanks on this page with the words called for. Then, using the words you have selected, fill in the blank spaces in the story.

Now you've created your own hilarious MAD LIBS® game!

WHO'S THAT DOG?, PART 3

NOUN_____

ADJECTIVE_____

ANIMAL (PLURAL)_____

NOUN_____

NOUN_____

PART OF THE BODY_____

NOUN_____

PART OF THE BODY_____

NOUN_____

PLURAL NOUN_____

VERB ENDING IN "ING"_____

PLURAL NOUN_____

PART OF THE BODY_____

NOUN_____

PLURAL NOUN_____

A few more dog breeds to brighten your _____!
NOUN

Yorkshire terrier: Yorkies may be small, but they are brave and _____.
ADJECTIVE

Yorkies were originally bred to hunt _____ in _____
ANIMAL (PLURAL)   NOUN

factories!

Doberman pinscher: The Doberman is a muscular _____. With
NOUN

its intelligent _____, the Doberman is often trained as a police
PART OF THE BODY

_____.
NOUN

Shih tzu: The shih tzu has a long and luxurious _____. This
PART OF THE BODY

playful _____ is usually friendly toward all _____.
NOUN   PLURAL NOUN

Australian shepherd: Aussies are very energetic and require daily

_____ to be happy. They are great at herding crowds of
VERB ENDING IN "ING"

_____ on the farm.
PLURAL NOUN

Pomeranian: The Pomeranian has a big, fluffy _____ to match
PART OF THE BODY

its outgoing _____. This intelligent little dog loves to please its
NOUN

_____.
PLURAL NOUN

MAD LIBS® is fun to play with friends, but you can also play it by yourself! To begin with, DO NOT look at the story on the page below. Fill in the blanks on this page with the words called for. Then, using the words you have selected, fill in the blank spaces in the story.

Now you've created your own hilarious MAD LIBS® game!

POOCH PALACE

ADJECTIVE _____

ANIMAL _____

NOUN _____

TYPE OF LIQUID _____

ADJECTIVE _____

PART OF THE BODY _____

OCCUPATION _____

NOUN _____

SILLY WORD _____

PART OF THE BODY _____

A PLACE _____

PART OF THE BODY _____

NOUN _____

PLURAL NOUN _____

MAD LIBS
POOCH PALACE

Welcome to the _____ Pooch Palace, the dog spa for all your
     ADJECTIVE

grooming needs! Below is our spa menu. How do you want to pamper your

_____ today?
 ANIMAL

- **Paw-dicure:** We'll not only trim your _____'s nails, we'll paint
          NOUN

  them with a coat of _____ so your pup looks _____
       TYPE OF LIQUID   ADJECTIVE

  and stylish.

- **Pup massage:** If your dog is in need of some rest and relaxation,

  a/an _____ massage might be just what the _____
    PART OF THE BODY   OCCUPATION

  ordered!

- **Doggy 'do:** Is your _____ looking shaggy? Our renowned
         NOUN

  stylist, Pierre _____, gives the best _____-cut
       SILLY WORD   PART OF THE BODY

  this side of (the) _____.
       A PLACE

- **Fur dye:** If you've ever wanted your dog's _____ to match
            PART OF THE BODY

  the color of your favorite _____, look no further. The Pooch
        NOUN

  Palace will make all your _____ come true!
        PLURAL NOUN

MAD LIBS® is fun to play with friends, but you can also play it by yourself! To begin with, DO NOT look at the story on the page below. Fill in the blanks on this page with the words called for. Then, using the words you have selected, fill in the blank spaces in the story.

Now you've created your own hilarious MAD LIBS® game!

HOMEWARD BOUND

A PLACE _____

ADJECTIVE _____

PERSON IN ROOM (FEMALE) _____

NUMBER _____

VERB (PAST TENSE) _____

PERSON IN ROOM _____

PART OF THE BODY (PLURAL) _____

NOUN _____

ADJECTIVE _____

NOUN _____

NOUN _____

PERSON IN ROOM _____

TYPE OF LIQUID _____

ADJECTIVE _____

MAD LIBS
HOMEWARD BOUND

In (the) _____ today, one _____ family was reunited with
$\qquad$ A PLACE $\qquad$ ADJECTIVE

their beloved dog, _____, who made her way home after
$\qquad$ PERSON IN ROOM (FEMALE)

being missing for _____ days. "She just showed up on our front
$\qquad$ NUMBER

doorstep this morning and _____," said _____. "We
$\qquad$ VERB (PAST TENSE) $\qquad$ PERSON IN ROOM

couldn't believe our _____." The family dog disappeared
$\qquad$ PART OF THE BODY (PLURAL)

after leaving the family's front yard to chase after a wild _____ one
$\qquad$ NOUN

afternoon, and the family has been worried _____ ever since. They
$\qquad$ ADJECTIVE

put up "lost _____" posters all over the neighborhood, and even
$\qquad$ NOUN

put a/an _____ in the local newspaper. "We have no idea where
$\qquad$ NOUN

she's been all this time," said _____. "We're just happier than
$\qquad$ PERSON IN ROOM

a pig in _____ that she's home again. We can't wait to spoil her
$\qquad$ TYPE OF LIQUID

_____."
$\qquad$ ADJECTIVE

MAD LIBS® is fun to play with friends, but you can also play it by yourself! To begin with, DO NOT look at the story on the page below. Fill in the blanks on this page with the words called for. Then, using the words you have selected, fill in the blank spaces in the story.

Now you've created your own hilarious MAD LIBS® game!

WONDER DOG

VERB _____

ADJECTIVE _____

PART OF THE BODY (PLURAL) _____

ADJECTIVE _____

NOUN _____

PART OF THE BODY _____

VERB ENDING IN "ING" _____

ADJECTIVE _____

PART OF THE BODY (PLURAL) _____

ADVERB _____

NOUN _____

ADJECTIVE _____

PLURAL NOUN _____

ADJECTIVE _____

ADJECTIVE _____

ADVERB _____

VERB _____

MAD LIBS®
WONDER DOG

Lots of dogs can sit, stay, and _____. But not many can do these
                  VERB

_____ tricks!
ADJECTIVE

- **Play dead:** When you say, "Bang! Bang!" some dogs will roll onto their

_____ and act _____. This act is sure to
PART OF THE BODY (PLURAL)   ADJECTIVE

tickle your funny _____.
               NOUN

- **Dance:** Your dog may know how to wag its _____ to
                       PART OF THE BODY

the beat, but can it dance like nobody's _____?
                      VERB ENDING IN "ING"

A dog that knows this _____ trick can stand on its hind
              ADJECTIVE

_____ and spin around _____!
PART OF THE BODY (PLURAL)   ADVERB

- **Bring my slippers:** Feeling lazy and don't want to get out of your

comfy _____? Ask your dog to do it! If your dog knows this
       NOUN

_____ trick, say, "Bring my slippers," and your dog will bring
ADJECTIVE

your _____ to you!
   PLURAL NOUN

- **Jump rope:** If your dog knows this _____ trick, grab a/an
                     ADJECTIVE

_____ rope and a partner, swing the rope _____,
ADJECTIVE   ADVERB

and your dog will _____ over it again and again!
            VERB

MAD LIBS® is fun to play with friends, but you can also play it by yourself! To begin with, DO NOT look at the story on the page below. Fill in the blanks on this page with the words called for. Then, using the words you have selected, fill in the blank spaces in the story.

Now you've created your own hilarious MAD LIBS® game!

DOG'S DELIGHT

VERB ENDING IN "S" _____

PART OF THE BODY _____

ADJECTIVE _____

PLURAL NOUN _____

ANIMAL _____

VERB _____

VERB _____

PLURAL NOUN _____

NOUN _____

PLURAL NOUN _____

NOUN _____

NOUN _____

NOUN _____

PLURAL NOUN _____

NOUN _____

ADJECTIVE _____

PART OF THE BODY _____

NOUN _____

MAD LIBS®
DOG'S DELIGHT

You know your dog is happy when it _____ and wags its
VERB ENDING IN "S"

_____ back and forth. If you want your dog to be _____
PART OF THE BODY   ADJECTIVE

as a clam at all times, try any of the following _____. It's a countdown
PLURAL NOUN

of your _____'s favorite things!
ANIMAL

5. **Walks:** Though some dogs would rather stay home and _____,
VERB

most dogs love to go for walks to _____ on fire hydrants and sniff
VERB

_____.
PLURAL NOUN

4. **Naps:** Dogs love to curl up on a/an _____ and dream about
NOUN

_____—especially if they're cuddling with their favorite
PLURAL NOUN

_____.
NOUN

3. **Playtime:** Fidos love to play fetch with a/an _____ or run around
NOUN

chasing a/an _____. Sometimes, _____ just wanna
NOUN   PLURAL NOUN

have fun!

2. **Food:** Whether it's a can of dog _____ or _____ table
NOUN   ADJECTIVE

scraps, dogs love to eat. The way to a dog's heart is definitely through its

_____!
PART OF THE BODY

1. **You!:** After all, a dog is a/an _____'s best friend.
NOUN

MAD LIBS® is fun to play with friends, but you can also play it by yourself! To begin with, DO NOT look at the story on the page below. Fill in the blanks on this page with the words called for. Then, using the words you have selected, fill in the blank spaces in the story.

Now you've created your own hilarious MAD LIBS® game!

WHO'S THAT DOG?, PART 4

VERB _____

COLOR _____

NOUN _____

VERB ENDING IN "ING" _____

NOUN _____

PART OF THE BODY _____

VERB _____

PART OF THE BODY (PLURAL) _____

A PLACE _____

NUMBER _____

ADJECTIVE _____

VERB _____

ADJECTIVE _____

PLURAL NOUN _____

A PLACE _____

ADJECTIVE _____

A final few furry dog breeds for you to love and _____ :

VERB

Collie: The brown and _____ collie is a friendly family _____ ,

COLOR _NOUN_

known for its grace and elegance when _____ .

VERB ENDING IN "ING"

Dalmatian: This black-and-white _____ is the only dog breed

NOUN

with spots on its _____ . They have lots of energy and need to

PART OF THE BODY

_____ a lot.

VERB

Pembroke Welsh corgi: The corgi is known for its very short

_____ and stout body. The queen of (the) _____

PART OF THE BODY (PLURAL) _A PLACE_

owns _____ corgis!

NUMBER

Miniature schnauzer: The miniature schnauzer may be small, but it is

a/an _____ guard dog, and will _____ at the sign of any

ADJECTIVE _VERB_

_____ intruder.

ADJECTIVE

St. Bernard: The St. Bernard was originally used to hunt for _____

PLURAL NOUN

during snowstorms in (the) _____ . They are very gentle and

A PLACE

_____ .

ADJECTIVE

MAD LIBS® is fun to play with friends, but you can also play it by yourself! To begin with, DO NOT look at the story on the page below. Fill in the blanks on this page with the words called for. Then, using the words you have selected, fill in the blank spaces in the story.

Now you've created your own hilarious MAD LIBS® game!

LET'S GO FOR A RIDE!

PERSON IN ROOM _____

PART OF THE BODY (PLURAL) _____

PART OF THE BODY (PLURAL) _____

ADJECTIVE _____

NOUN _____

NOUN _____

PART OF THE BODY _____

PLURAL NOUN _____

PART OF THE BODY (PLURAL) _____

PART OF THE BODY _____

ADJECTIVE _____

ADVERB _____

NOUN _____

PERSON IN ROOM _____

EXCLAMATION _____

NOUN _____

MAD LIBS®
LET'S GO FOR A RIDE!

"_____, come!" I hear my owner call out. My _____
PERSON IN ROOM   PART OF THE BODY (PLURAL)

perk up—is that the sound of the garage door opening? Suddenly, I am excited

from my head to my _____. Can it be? Am I going
PART OF THE BODY (PLURAL)

for a/an _____ car ride? I bound to the door, where I see my owner
ADJECTIVE

getting into the car. She pats the seat. "Come on, _____!" she calls.
NOUN

This is the best _____ ever! I hop happily into the front seat and
NOUN

immediately stick my _____ out of the car window. We drive
PART OF THE BODY

away down the street, passing houses and mailboxes and _____.
PLURAL NOUN

I can feel the wind in my _____ and the sun on my
PART OF THE BODY (PLURAL)

_____, and everything smells _____. *Where are we*
PART OF THE BODY   ADJECTIVE

going? I wonder _____. So you can imagine my _____ as
ADVERB   NOUN

we pulled into the parking lot of Dr. _____'s office. *We're going to*
PERSON IN ROOM

the vet? _____! This is the worst _____ ever!
EXCLAMATION   NOUN

MAD LIBS® is fun to play with friends, but you can also play it by yourself! To begin with, DO NOT look at the story on the page below. Fill in the blanks on this page with the words called for. Then, using the words you have selected, fill in the blank spaces in the story.

Now you've created your own hilarious MAD LIBS® game!

FAMOUS FIDOS: SCOOBY-DOO

NOUN _____

NOUN _____

PERSON IN ROOM _____

FIRST NAME _____

NOUN _____

ADJECTIVE _____

PLURAL NOUN _____

PLURAL NOUN _____

SAME PLURAL NOUN _____

PLURAL NOUN _____

PLURAL NOUN _____

ADJECTIVE _____

SILLY WORD _____

Scooby-Doo is the star of the animated television _____ *Scooby-*
NOUN

Doo, Where Are You! Scooby-Doo, also known as Scooby, is a talking

_____ who solves mysteries along with four teenagers named Shaggy,
NOUN

Daphne, _____, and _____. Scooby-Doo, a
PERSON IN ROOM   FIRST NAME

Great _____, belongs to his _____ friend, Shaggy. Much
NOUN   ADJECTIVE

like Shaggy, Scooby is scared of _____ and is always hungry for
PLURAL NOUN

cookies called Scooby _____. Luckily, the prospect of eating Scooby
PLURAL NOUN

_____ and keeping his friends safe from _____ helps
SAME PLURAL NOUN   PLURAL NOUN

Scooby to be brave and stand up to scary _____. Scooby and his
PLURAL NOUN

friends always solve the _____ mystery, and Scooby always ends each
ADJECTIVE

episode by saying "_____-dooby-doo!"
SILLY WORD

MAD LIBS® is fun to play with friends, but you can also play it by yourself! To begin with, DO NOT look at the story on the page below. Fill in the blanks on this page with the words called for. Then, using the words you have selected, fill in the blank spaces in the story.

Now you've created your own hilarious MAD LIBS® game!

DOGS VERSUS CATS

ADJECTIVE _____

ADJECTIVE _____

PART OF THE BODY _____

NUMBER _____

ADJECTIVE _____

PLURAL NOUN _____

NOUN _____

PLURAL NOUN _____

PART OF THE BODY (PLURAL) _____

NOUN _____

PART OF THE BODY _____

NOUN _____

NOUN _____

NOUN _____

SAME NOUN _____

ADJECTIVE _____

NOUN _____

MAD LIBS®
DOGS VERSUS CATS

Which are better, _____ cats or _____ dogs? Anyone with
ADJECTIVE   ADJECTIVE

half a/an _____ knows that dogs are _____ times better
PART OF THE BODY   NUMBER

than cats. Dogs are _____ companions, while cats only care about
ADJECTIVE

their own _____. Dogs are loyal to their _____, but cats
PLURAL NOUN   NOUN

will love whoever gives them _____ to eat. Dogs like to have their
PLURAL NOUN

_____ rubbed, while cats will bite your _____
PART OF THE BODY (PLURAL)   NOUN

if you try to put a/an _____ on them. Most dogs love going for
PART OF THE BODY

rides in a/an _____, but cats just get sick all over your favorite
NOUN

_____. Dogs love to play fetch with a/an _____, but if
NOUN   NOUN

you throw a/an _____ for a cat, it will just look at you like you're
SAME NOUN

_____. All in all, when it comes to dogs versus cats, only the dog is
ADJECTIVE

truly man's best _____.
NOUN

MAD LIBS® is fun to play with friends, but you can also play it by yourself! To begin with, DO NOT look at the story on the page below. Fill in the blanks on this page with the words called for. Then, using the words you have selected, fill in the blank spaces in the story.

Now you've created your own hilarious MAD LIBS® game!

FOREVER HOME

LAST NAME _____

NOUN _____

ADJECTIVE _____

ADJECTIVE _____

PART OF THE BODY (PLURAL) _____

COLOR _____

PART OF THE BODY _____

ADJECTIVE _____

NOUN _____

A PLACE _____

ADJECTIVE _____

PLURAL NOUN _____

ADJECTIVE _____

ADJECTIVE _____

PART OF THE BODY _____

EXCLAMATION _____

ADVERB _____

MAD LIBS
FOREVER HOME

When the _____ family went to the animal shelter,
LAST NAME

they never knew they'd find a/an _____ like Rex. The family
NOUN

looked at all the dogs before making this very _____ decision.
ADJECTIVE

Sure, the puppies were cute and _____, but one older dog stole the
ADJECTIVE

family's _____. His name was Rex, and with his fuzzy
PART OF THE BODY (PLURAL)

_____ fur, his crooked _____, and his _____
COLOR   PART OF THE BODY   ADJECTIVE

personality, the family knew they'd found their new _____. Plus, by
NOUN

bringing Rex back to (the) _____ with them, they saved his life. Now
A PLACE

Rex would have a/an _____ place to sleep, _____ to eat, and
ADJECTIVE   PLURAL NOUN

a/an _____ family to call his own. And Rex would more than repay
ADJECTIVE

his family with lots of _____ wet kisses on the _____
ADJECTIVE   PART OF THE BODY

and unconditional love. _____! Rex had found his forever home,
EXCLAMATION

and they all lived _____ ever after.
ADVERB

INSTRUCTIONS

MAD LIBS® is a game for people who don't like games!
It can be played by one, two, three, four, or forty.

• RIDICULOUSLY SIMPLE DIRECTIONS

In this tablet you will find stories containing blank spaces where words are left out.
One player, the READER, selects one of these stories. The READER does not tell anyone
what the story is about. Instead, he/she asks the other players, the WRITERS, to give
him/her words. These words are used to fill in the blank spaces in the story.

• TO PLAY

The READER asks each WRITER in turn to call out a word—an adjective or a noun or
whatever the space calls for—and uses them to fill in the blank spaces in the story. The
result is a MAD LIBS® game.

When the READER then reads the completed MAD LIBS® game to the other players,
they will discover that they have written a story that is fantastic, screamingly funny,
shocking, silly, crazy, or just plain dumb—depending upon which words each WRITER
called out.

• EXAMPLE (*Before* and *After*)

"_____!" he said _____
　　　　　EXCLAMATION　　　　　　　　　　　　　　　　ADVERB

as he jumped into his convertible _____ and
　　　　　　　　　　　　　　　　　　　　　　　NOUN

drove off with his _____ wife.
　　　　　　　　　　ADJECTIVE

"_____OUCH_____!" he said _____HAPPILY_____
　　　　EXCLAMATION　　　　　　　　　　　　　ADVERB

as he jumped into his convertible _____CAT_____ and
　　　　　　　　　　　　　　　　　　　　NOUN

drove off with his _____BRAVE_____ wife.
　　　　　　　　　　ADJECTIVE

QUICK REVIEW

In case you have forgotten what adjectives, adverbs, nouns, and verbs are, here is a quick review:

An ADJECTIVE describes something or somebody. *Lumpy, soft, ugly, messy,* and *short* are adjectives.

An ADVERB tells how something is done. It modifies a verb and usually ends in "ly." *Modestly, stupidly, greedily,* and *carefully* are adverbs.

A NOUN is the name of a person, place, or thing. *Sidewalk, umbrella, bridle, bathtub,* and *nose* are nouns.

A VERB is an action word. *Run, pitch, jump,* and *swim* are verbs. Put the verbs in past tense if the directions say PAST TENSE. *Ran, pitched, jumped,* and *swam* are verbs in the past tense.

When we ask for A PLACE, we mean any sort of place: a country or city *(Spain, Cleveland)* or a room *(bathroom, kitchen).*

An EXCLAMATION or SILLY WORD is any sort of funny sound, gasp, grunt, or outcry, like *Wow!, Ouch!, Whomp!, Ick!,* and *Gadzooks!*

When we ask for specific words, like a NUMBER, a COLOR, an ANIMAL, or a PART OF THE BODY, we mean a word that is one of those things, like *seven, blue, horse,* or *head.*

When we ask for a PLURAL, it means more than one. For example, *cat* pluralized is *cats.*

MAD LIBS® is fun to play with friends, but you can also play it by yourself! To begin with, DO NOT look at the story on the page below. Fill in the blanks on this page with the words called for. Then, using the words you have selected, fill in the blank spaces in the story.

Now you've created your own hilarious MAD LIBS® game!

HORSE SENSE

ADJECTIVE _____

VERB ENDING IN "ING" _____

NUMBER _____

PLURAL NOUN _____

ANIMAL (PLURAL) _____

PART OF THE BODY (PLURAL) _____

PLURAL NOUN _____

TYPE OF FOOD _____

ADJECTIVE _____

NUMBER _____

VERB (PAST TENSE) _____

VERB _____

ADJECTIVE _____

OCCUPATION (PLURAL) _____

VERB ENDING IN "ING" _____

EXCLAMATION _____

ADJECTIVE _____

PART OF THE BODY _____

MAD LIBS
HORSE SENSE

Horses are some of the most _____ animals on the planet.
ADJECTIVE

They are natural runners and jumpers—quarter horses have been clocked

_____ at fifty-five miles per hour, and the world's record
VERB ENDING IN "ING"

for a horse jump is eight feet, _____ inches! Traditionally social
NUMBER

_____, horses live in a herd with other _____. They can
PLURAL NOUN   ANIMAL (PLURAL)

sleep lying down or take a nap standing on their _____.
PART OF THE BODY (PLURAL)

All horses are _____, meaning they only eat _____.
PLURAL NOUN   TYPE OF FOOD

Humans and horses have a/an _____ bond. The first wild horses
ADJECTIVE

were domesticated around _____ years ago. Since then, horses
NUMBER

have bravely _____ soldiers into battle, helped farmers
VERB (PAST TENSE)

_____ their fields, sprinted in _____ races for royalty, and
VERB   ADJECTIVE

been loyal partners for _____ on patrol. Today, many people
OCCUPATION (PLURAL)

enjoy _____ on horses for pleasure or as a form of therapy.
VERB ENDING IN "ING"

So, _____! The _____ power of horses will gallop its way
EXCLAMATION   ADJECTIVE

into your _____!
PART OF THE BODY

MAD LIBS® is fun to play with friends, but you can also play it by yourself! To begin with, DO NOT look at the story on the page below. Fill in the blanks on this page with the words called for. Then, using the words you have selected, fill in the blank spaces in the story.

Now you've created your own hilarious MAD LIBS® game!

EQUINE ETIQUETTE

SILLY WORD _____

ADJECTIVE _____

FIRST NAME _____

VERB _____

VERB _____

ADJECTIVE _____

ADVERB _____

ADJECTIVE _____

SOMETHING ALIVE _____

PART OF THE BODY _____

VERB _____

ARTICLE OF CLOTHING (PLURAL) _____

PART OF THE BODY _____

NUMBER _____

EXCLAMATION _____

ADJECTIVE _____

TYPE OF FOOD (PLURAL) _____

PART OF THE BODY _____

MAD LIBS®
EQUINE ETIQUETTE

_____, partner! You get to take your _____ horse,
　　SILLY WORD　　　　　　　　　　　　　　　　　　　ADJECTIVE

_____, out for a trail ride today! Before you _____ in the
　FIRST NAME　　　　　　　　　　　　　　　　　　　　　VERB

saddle, let's review basic horse safety rules:

- Walk, don't _____. Horses have a/an _____
　　　　　　　　　VERB　　　　　　　　　　　　　　　　　ADJECTIVE

  "startle" reflex, so approach _____ and greet them with a/an
　　　　　　　　　　　　　　　　ADVERB

  _____ voice.
　　ADJECTIVE

- Don't stand directly behind a/an _____. A horse's eyes are
　　　　　　　　　　　　　　　SOMETHING ALIVE

  located on the side of its _____, making them likely to kick
　　　　　　　　　　　PART OF THE BODY

  anything they cannot _____ clearly.
　　　　　　　　　VERB

- Always wear _____ on your feet, in case your horse
　　　　　ARTICLE OF CLOTHING (PLURAL)

  stomps on your _____. Horses can weigh up to _____
　　　　　PART OF THE BODY　　　　　　　　　　　　　NUMBER

  pounds—_____!
　　　　EXCLAMATION

- It's _____ to feed your horse some treats. They love
　　　ADJECTIVE

  _____! Offer treats using a flat _____ so
　TYPE OF FOOD (PLURAL)　　　　　　　　　PART OF THE BODY

  your fingers don't get nibbled by your hangry horse.

MAD LIBS® is fun to play with friends, but you can also play it by yourself! To begin with, DO NOT look at the story on the page below. Fill in the blanks on this page with the words called for. Then, using the words you have selected, fill in the blank spaces in the story.

Now you've created your own hilarious MAD LIBS® game!

HORSE OF A DIFFERENT COLOR

ADJECTIVE _____

PART OF THE BODY (PLURAL) _____

ARTICLE OF CLOTHING (PLURAL) _____

PLURAL NOUN _____

ADJECTIVE _____

ADJECTIVE _____

COLOR _____

COLOR _____

FIRST NAME _____

NOUN _____

PERSON IN ROOM _____

COUNTRY _____

ANIMAL _____

VERB ENDING IN "ING" _____

PART OF THE BODY _____

PART OF THE BODY (PLURAL) _____

VERB _____

Horses come in many colors and can have _____ markings on their
_____ that look like spots, _____,
PART OF THE BODY (PLURAL)   ARTICLE OF CLOTHING (PLURAL)

or _____. The combinations are _____! The most
PLURAL NOUN   ADJECTIVE

_____ horse coat is called bay, which means the horse has a/an
ADJECTIVE

_____ body with a/an _____ mane. Legendary
COLOR   COLOR

racehorse _____ was a bay. The palomino, with its gleaming
FIRST NAME

white mane and golden-blond _____, is easily recognizable! Mister
NOUN

_____, who starred in his own TV show, was a palomino.
PERSON IN ROOM

Appaloosas were first bred in _____, and they are identified
COUNTRY

by the _____-like spots covering their bodies. A horse is
ANIMAL

_____ socks when it has a white marking on its legs, from
VERB ENDING IN "ING"

its hoof to just above the _____. Horses with white markings on
PART OF THE BODY

their foreheads between their _____ are said to have
PART OF THE BODY (PLURAL)

stars. (Pro tip: Many horses love it when you _____ them there!)
VERB

MAD LIBS® is fun to play with friends, but you can also play it by yourself! To begin with, DO NOT look at the story on the page below. Fill in the blanks on this page with the words called for. Then, using the words you have selected, fill in the blank spaces in the story.

Now you've created your own hilarious MAD LIBS® game!

TRICK PONY

ADJECTIVE _____

NOUN _____

ANIMAL (PLURAL) _____

NUMBER _____

PLURAL NOUN _____

ADJECTIVE _____

VERB _____

ANIMAL (PLURAL) _____

A PLACE _____

VERB ENDING IN "ING" _____

VERB _____

NOUN _____

ADJECTIVE _____

NOUN _____

VERB ENDING IN "ING" _____

ADJECTIVE _____

VERB _____

EXCLAMATION _____

It's a/an _____ morning here on the Circle _____ Ranch,
      ADJECTIVE   NOUN

and we've got cattle to round up! Luckily, the ranch has some whip-smart cow

ponies who know how to wrangle a herd of _____ . These
                                        ANIMAL (PLURAL)

_____-legged heroes can do amazing _____ and will never
   NUMBER   PLURAL NOUN

steer you in the _____ direction. Our cattle horses are trained to
                    ADJECTIVE

_____ their riders in moving large groups of _____ from
   VERB   ANIMAL (PLURAL)

one _____ to another. And if a new calf is _____
    A PLACE   VERB ENDING IN "ING"

away, don't worry, ranch horses have "cow sense" and can _____ up
                                             VERB

the straggler and guide it back to the _____ . They're independent
                              NOUN

thinkers and can make _____ decisions without direction from their
                    ADJECTIVE

riders! Working cattle horses are known for being able to stop on a/an

_____ , _____ at high speeds, and sustaining
  NOUN   VERB ENDING IN "ING"

_____ rides. These working horses can even _____
  ADJECTIVE   VERB

backward. _____ , partner!
      EXCLAMATION

MAD LIBS® is fun to play with friends, but you can also play it by yourself! To begin with, DO NOT look at the story on the page below. Fill in the blanks on this page with the words called for. Then, using the words you have selected, fill in the blank spaces in the story.

Now you've created your own hilarious MAD LIBS® game!

GAIT AND SWITCH

ADJECTIVE _____

VERB _____

ADJECTIVE _____

VERB ENDING IN "ING" _____

ANIMAL (PLURAL) _____

VERB _____

ADJECTIVE _____

NOUN _____

VERB ENDING IN "S" _____

NOUN _____

NUMBER _____

PLURAL NOUN _____

NOUN _____

VERB _____

VERB ENDING IN "ING" _____

NOUN _____

MAD LIBS®
GAIT AND SWITCH

Horses have distinct ways of walking (talk about _____ footwork!)
ADJECTIVE

known as gaits. Different breeds of horses can be taught to _____
VERB

highly-specialized types of movement—think _____ kicking
ADJECTIVE

steps and skipping strides that resemble _____! But all
VERB ENDING IN "ING"

_____ naturally know how to _____ the four
ANIMAL (PLURAL)   VERB

_____ gaits. The gallop is a fast-paced _____ that really
ADJECTIVE   NOUN

_____! Its four-beat rhythm can win races, deliver the
VERB ENDING IN "S"

_____, and even help bad guys make quick getaways. The walk is
NOUN

a/an _____-beat gait. Horses traveling at this slow pace can cover fifty
NUMBER

_____ in a day. A trot is a common gait that is faster than a walk, but
PLURAL NOUN

slower than a/an _____. Riders either _____ or post—
NOUN   VERB

rise and sit in time—to its rhythmic beats. Horses who canter are said to

resemble the motion of toy _____ horses. This three-beat
VERB ENDING IN "ING"

rhythm is slower than a/an _____ and faster than a trot!
NOUN

MAD LIBS® is fun to play with friends, but you can also play it by yourself! To begin with, DO NOT look at the story on the page below. Fill in the blanks on this page with the words called for. Then, using the words you have selected, fill in the blank spaces in the story.

Now you've created your own hilarious MAD LIBS® game!

POEM FROM
A CAROUSEL HORSE

ADJECTIVE _____

ADJECTIVE _____

PLURAL NOUN _____

ANIMAL _____

VERB _____

OCCUPATION (PLURAL) _____

PLURAL NOUN _____

VERB _____

ADJECTIVE _____

NOUN _____

ADJECTIVE _____

PLURAL NOUN _____

SOMETHING ALIVE (PLURAL) _____

VERB _____

VERB ENDING IN "ING" _____

ADJECTIVE _____

I was carved to look _____ and _____,
                         ADJECTIVE   ADJECTIVE

decorated with _____ like my brothers.
                  PLURAL NOUN

In my life as a carousel _____,
                              ANIMAL

I _____ _____ and their mothers!
      VERB   OCCUPATION (PLURAL)

First, organs piped peppy _____ all day,
                              PLURAL NOUN

playing tunes on this merry-_____-round.
                                 VERB

Now the _____ music is digital,
            ADJECTIVE

but still has a magical _____.
                            NOUN

_____ colors, bright _____, these are the sights
   ADJECTIVE   PLURAL NOUN

that get the _____ in a tizzy.
               SOMETHING ALIVE (PLURAL)

Kids _____ up and down, _____ around,
         VERB   VERB ENDING IN "ING"

and crying, "This ride is making me _____!"
                                         ADJECTIVE

MAD LIBS® is fun to play with friends, but you can also play it by yourself! To begin with, DO NOT look at the story on the page below. Fill in the blanks on this page with the words called for. Then, using the words you have selected, fill in the blank spaces in the story.

Now you've created your own hilarious MAD LIBS® game!

HEART OF A CHAMPION

ADJECTIVE _____

A PLACE _____

COLOR _____

NOUN _____

ANIMAL _____

PLURAL NOUN _____

PLURAL NOUN _____

EXCLAMATION _____

NUMBER _____

NOUN _____

VEHICLE _____

FIRST NAME _____

ADJECTIVE _____

VERB (PAST TENSE) _____

NUMBER _____

NOUN _____

NOUN _____

Secretariat was one of the most _____ racehorses in history.
ADJECTIVE

The stallion was born in (the) _____ and nicknamed "Big
A PLACE

_____" for his reddish-brown coat. Among his many achievements
COLOR

was winning the Triple _____—considered the most difficult feat in
NOUN

_____ racing. He set many world _____ and still holds
ANIMAL   PLURAL NOUN

the best _____ ever for his Triple Crown wins. _____!
PLURAL NOUN   EXCLAMATION

Standing at _____ hands tall, Secretariat was known for his giant
NUMBER

_____ length. One of his galloping strides measured twenty-four
NOUN

feet—that's as long as a/an _____! _____ was also known
VEHICLE   FIRST NAME

for his near-perfect conformation—the shape and structure of his build. His

_____ legs and hindquarters made him a powerful athlete. It was
ADJECTIVE

later _____ that Secretariat's heart was more than _____
VERB (PAST TENSE)   NUMBER

times the size of an average racehorse's heart. With a heart that large,

Secretariat's body functioned like a well-oiled _____. He truly was
NOUN

a special horse with the _____ of a champion.
NOUN

MAD LIBS® is fun to play with friends, but you can also play it by yourself! To begin with, DO NOT look at the story on the page below. Fill in the blanks on this page with the words called for. Then, using the words you have selected, fill in the blank spaces in the story.

Now you've created your own hilarious MAD LIBS® game!

HOOFING IT

ANIMAL (PLURAL) _____

ARTICLE OF CLOTHING (PLURAL) _____

NOUN _____

ADJECTIVE _____

OCCUPATION (PLURAL) _____

SOMETHING ALIVE (PLURAL) _____

VERB _____

ADJECTIVE _____

ADVERB _____

VERB (PAST TENSE) _____

NUMBER _____

ADJECTIVE _____

NOUN _____

PART OF THE BODY (PLURAL) _____

VERB _____

PLURAL NOUN _____

ADJECTIVE _____

MAD LIBS®
HOOFING IT

Did you know _____ wear _____ on their
　　　　　　　ANIMAL (PLURAL)　　　　ARTICLE OF CLOTHING (PLURAL)

feet? We talked to a farrier—a/an _____ who specializes in equine
　　　　　　　　　　　　　　　　　　　NOUN

hoof and shoe care—to get the _____-down on this amazing
　　　　　　　　　　　　　　ADJECTIVE

profession. _____ love being around _____.
　　　　　OCCUPATION (PLURAL)　　　　　　SOMETHING ALIVE (PLURAL)

They can always tell when it's time to _____ new shoes for a horse.
　　　　　　　　　　　　　　　　　　VERB

But their work can be _____! They are _____ in danger
　　　　　　　　　ADJECTIVE　　　　　　　　ADVERB

of being _____ on. Even after _____ years on the job,
　　　VERB (PAST TENSE)　　　　　　　　NUMBER

farriers still get stepped on once in a while. So, they always wear _____
　　　　　　　　　　　　　　　　　　　　　　　　　　　　ADJECTIVE

boots and try to stay focused on their _____. A good farrier knows
　　　　　　　　　　　　　　　　　NOUN

that a horse's _____ are actually quite delicate. Depending
　　　　PART OF THE BODY (PLURAL)

on the type of work a horse does, shoes can _____ protection or help
　　　　　　　　　　　　　　　　　　　VERB

keep the horse's footing on loose _____. Plus, who doesn't love a/an
　　　　　　　　　　　　　　PLURAL NOUN

_____ pair of shoes!
　ADJECTIVE

MAD LIBS® is fun to play with friends, but you can also play it by yourself! To begin with, DO NOT look at the story on the page below. Fill in the blanks on this page with the words called for. Then, using the words you have selected, fill in the blank spaces in the story.

Now you've created your own hilarious MAD LIBS® game!

TACK TRUNK JUNK

VERB ENDING IN "ING" _____

ADJECTIVE _____

NOUN _____

PERSON IN ROOM _____

PLURAL NOUN _____

ADJECTIVE _____

COLOR _____

PART OF THE BODY _____

VERB _____

ANIMAL _____

VERB _____

NUMBER _____

NOUN _____

VERB ENDING IN "S" _____

VERB _____

ADJECTIVE _____

TYPE OF FOOD _____

MAD LIBS®
TACK TRUNK JUNK

Lueen loves horseback _____ and is beyond _____ to
VERB ENDING IN "ING"   ADJECTIVE

compete in the _____ racing competition! Let's pack her tack trunk
NOUN

so she and her horse, _____, have everything they need. Here
PERSON IN ROOM

are the _____ on her list:
PLURAL NOUN

- Lueen's _____ boots! These _____ and red beauties
  ADJECTIVE   COLOR

  keep Lueen's _____ securely in her stirrups.
  PART OF THE BODY

- A saddle is a definite must-_____. Barrel racing is a rodeo event
  VERB

  in which a/an _____ and rider _____ in a cloverleaf
  ANIMAL   VERB

  pattern around _____ barrels in the center of the ring. The fastest
  NUMBER

  _____ wins. Having a saddle that _____ snugly to
  NOUN   VERB ENDING IN "S"

  the horse's back helps Lueen stay on her horse.

- A girl's gotta _____! Lueen should pack some _____
  VERB   ADJECTIVE

  treats for herself and her steed. _____ slices, anyone?
  TYPE OF FOOD

MAD LIBS® is fun to play with friends, but you can also play it by yourself! To begin with, DO NOT look at the story on the page below. Fill in the blanks on this page with the words called for. Then, using the words you have selected, fill in the blank spaces in the story.

Now you've created your own hilarious MAD LIBS® game!

HORSE TRAINER WANTED

OCCUPATION _____

ANIMAL _____

ADJECTIVE _____

NOUN _____

VERB _____

TYPE OF CONTAINER _____

TYPE OF FOOD (PLURAL) _____

PART OF THE BODY _____

NUMBER _____

VERB ENDING IN "ING" _____

PLURAL NOUN _____

ADJECTIVE _____

NOUN _____

ADVERB _____

ARTICLE OF CLOTHING (PLURAL) _____

PLURAL NOUN _____

PART OF THE BODY _____

EXCLAMATION _____

MAD LIBS®
HORSE TRAINER WANTED

Seeking experienced horse _____ or _____ whisperer to
                                OCCUPATION   ANIMAL

break our beloved horse, Blue Lightning, of some _____ habits. Blue
                                                      ADJECTIVE

_____ won't let anyone _____ on him, even if they
       NOUN   VERB

give him a/an _____ full of _____. No
                 TYPE OF CONTAINER   TYPE OF FOOD (PLURAL)

one has managed to stay on this horse's _____ for more
                                              PART OF THE BODY

than _____ seconds. Other undesirable behaviors include
          NUMBER

_____ when being brushed and chewing on the other horses'
   VERB ENDING IN "ING"

leather _____. This often results in _____ . . . tummy
           PLURAL NOUN   ADJECTIVE

troubles. The brave _____ who takes this job will be paid
                          NOUN

_____ for their time. Please come dressed in waterproof
       ADVERB

_____ as Blue Lightning also has allergies that cause
   ARTICLE OF CLOTHING (PLURAL)

him to sneeze _____ all over your _____ when you least
                   PLURAL NOUN   PART OF THE BODY

expect it. _____!
              EXCLAMATION

MAD LIBS® is fun to play with friends, but you can also play it by yourself! To begin with, DO NOT look at the story on the page below. Fill in the blanks on this page with the words called for. Then, using the words you have selected, fill in the blank spaces in the story.

Now you've created your own hilarious MAD LIBS® game!

O PIONEERS

ADJECTIVE _____

ADJECTIVE _____

NOUN _____

VEHICLE _____

NUMBER _____

ADJECTIVE _____

VERB _____

PLURAL NOUN _____

NOUN _____

VERB _____

ANIMAL (PLURAL) _____

ADJECTIVE _____

VERB ENDING IN "ING" _____

SOMETHING ALIVE (PLURAL) _____

TYPE OF FOOD _____

A PLACE _____

NOUN _____

VERB _____

MAD LIBS®
O PIONEERS

Greetings from the dusty and _____ Oregon Trail. It's the year 1839,
ADJECTIVE

and I'm _____ _____, one of the horses pulling a
ADJECTIVE   NOUN

Conestoga _____ over _____ miles across the prairie from
VEHICLE   NUMBER

Missouri to Oregon. Let me tell you, it's been a/an _____ trip so far!
ADJECTIVE

We _____ our heavy wagon every day, come rain or _____.
VERB   PLURAL NOUN

Once, we had to park our wagons in the shape of a/an _____ to
NOUN

_____ ourselves from a pack of howling _____. But it's
VERB   ANIMAL (PLURAL)

not all _____. I like _____ in new places, and
ADJECTIVE   VERB ENDING IN "ING"

there's usually plenty of prairie _____ to nibble on. But
SOMETHING ALIVE (PLURAL)

sometimes I do miss eating buckets full of _____ and sleeping
TYPE OF FOOD

in a cozy _____. Until then, I guess I'll try to keep my head up and
A PLACE

just enjoy the _____. Onward we _____, Oregon or
NOUN   VERB

bust!

MAD LIBS® is fun to play with friends, but you can also play it by yourself! To begin with, DO NOT look at the story on the page below. Fill in the blanks on this page with the words called for. Then, using the words you have selected, fill in the blank spaces in the story.

Now you've created your own hilarious MAD LIBS® game!

HORSEPLAY

EXCLAMATION _____

VERB (PAST TENSE) _____

PLURAL NOUN _____

VERB ENDING IN "ING" _____

ANIMAL _____

ADJECTIVE _____

VERB ENDING IN "ING" _____

FIRST NAME _____

NOUN _____

VERB _____

VERB _____

COLOR _____

NOUN _____

VERB ENDING IN "ING" _____

PART OF THE BODY _____

ADJECTIVE _____

NOUN _____

NOUN _____

_____ for Hollywood! Horses have played roles in movies since
EXCLAMATION

the first silent films _____ in theaters about a hundred
VERB (PAST TENSE)

_____ ago. And not long after, horses were _____
PLURAL NOUN   VERB ENDING IN "ING"

in TV shows and outshining their costars. Known as "the smartest

_____ in the movies," Trigger was the _____ partner of
ANIMAL   ADJECTIVE

the famous _____ cowboy _____ Rogers. The
VERB ENDING IN "ING"   FIRST NAME

horse learned to sign his _____ with an *x*, _____ in a
NOUN   VERB

chair, and take a bow whenever he heard an audience _____. *Mister*
VERB

Ed was a black and _____ TV show about a talking _____.
COLOR   NOUN

To make it look like the horse was _____, trainers taught
VERB ENDING IN "ING"

him to move his lips whenever they touched his _____. The horse
PART OF THE BODY

was so _____ that he learned to move his lips on cue whenever
ADJECTIVE

his human co-_____ stopped talking! Lights, _____,
NOUN   NOUN

giddyap!

MAD LIBS® is fun to play with friends, but you can also play it by yourself! To begin with, DO NOT look at the story on the page below. Fill in the blanks on this page with the words called for. Then, using the words you have selected, fill in the blank spaces in the story.

Now you've created your own hilarious MAD LIBS® game!

STRAIGHT TO THE HORSE'S MOUTH

ADJECTIVE _____

SOMETHING ALIVE (PLURAL) _____

ANIMAL (PLURAL) _____

PART OF THE BODY _____

NOUN _____

TYPE OF FOOD (PLURAL) _____

VERB _____

ADJECTIVE _____

TYPE OF FOOD _____

TYPE OF CONTAINER _____

NUMBER _____

ADVERB _____

PART OF THE BODY (PLURAL) _____

NOUN _____

NUMBER _____

COLOR _____

VERB _____

Natural vegetarians, horses mostly eat a/an _____ diet of pasture
ADJECTIVE

grass and bales of _____ . It turns out, hay really IS for
SOMETHING ALIVE (PLURAL)

_____! However, many horses have a sweet _____!
ANIMAL (PLURAL)   PART OF THE BODY

Here's a recipe for a dozen _____ -covered _____
NOUN   TYPE OF FOOD (PLURAL)

that your faithful steed is sure to _____ .
VERB

Ingredients: 1 _____ apple, 1 chopped _____ ,
ADJECTIVE   TYPE OF FOOD

1 _____ of molasses, and _____ cups of oats
TYPE OF CONTAINER   NUMBER

Instructions: Mix the ingredients _____ until the mixture is gooey
ADVERB

enough to stick to your _____! Place large spoonfuls
PART OF THE BODY (PLURAL)

on a baking _____ . Bake at _____ degrees for 30 minutes
NOUN   NUMBER

or until golden _____ . Let cool and watch your favorite horse
COLOR

_____!
VERB

MAD LIBS® is fun to play with friends, but you can also play it by yourself! To begin with, DO NOT look at the story on the page below. Fill in the blanks on this page with the words called for. Then, using the words you have selected, fill in the blank spaces in the story.

Now you've created your own hilarious MAD LIBS® game!

STABLE STABLEMATES

VERB _____

SOMETHING ALIVE (PLURAL) _____

PERSON IN ROOM _____

SILLY WORD _____

NOUN _____

ADJECTIVE _____

VERB ENDING IN "ING" _____

ADJECTIVE _____

NOUN _____

EXCLAMATION _____

VERB _____

ADJECTIVE _____

PART OF THE BODY _____

NOUN _____

VERB _____

PART OF THE BODY _____

SAME PERSON IN ROOM _____

NOUN _____

MAD LIBS
STABLE STABLEMATES

Horses are more relaxed when they _____ with other barnyard
VERB
_____ . Here's what a conversation between a scaredy-horse
SOMETHING ALIVE (PLURAL)
and a goat named _____ might sound like.
PERSON IN ROOM

Horse: _____ !! What is that thing hiding in the _____ ?
SILLY WORD   NOUN

Goat: Relax. It's just a/an _____ blanket _____
ADJECTIVE   VERB ENDING IN "ING"
in the wind.

Horse: Oh, _____ me. I thought it was a giant _____
ADJECTIVE   NOUN
coming to get us while we— _____ !! Did you _____
EXCLAMATION   VERB
that?!

Goat: Okay, now you're being _____ . That was just your
ADJECTIVE
_____ brushing up against the stall _____ . You have
PART OF THE BODY   NOUN
got to _____ down or you'll never get any shut- _____
VERB   PART OF THE BODY
before your show tomorrow.

Horse: You're right, _____ . Do you think you could read me a
SAME PERSON IN ROOM
bedtime _____ ?
NOUN

MAD LIBS® is fun to play with friends, but you can also play it by yourself! To begin with, DO NOT look at the story on the page below. Fill in the blanks on this page with the words called for. Then, using the words you have selected, fill in the blank spaces in the story.

Now you've created your own hilarious MAD LIBS® game!

WHICH TYPE OF HORSE ARE YOU?

PLURAL NOUN_____

VERB_____

ADJECTIVE_____

PLURAL NOUN_____

ADJECTIVE_____

COLOR_____

ADJECTIVE_____

OCCUPATION_____

VERB_____

NOUN_____

ADJECTIVE_____

NOUN_____

A PLACE_____

PART OF THE BODY_____

ADJECTIVE_____

NOUN_____

NOUN_____

VERB_____

MAD LIBS®
WHICH TYPE OF HORSE
ARE YOU?

Different horse breeds have distinct personality _____. Which
                                              PLURAL NOUN

breed do you like, and what does it _____ about you?
                                        VERB

- **Clydesdale:** You're a/an _____ giant. You can pull heavy
                                 ADJECTIVE

  _____ and are generally in _____ spirits. You also wear
   PLURAL NOUN   ADJECTIVE

  supercool _____ socks and have _____ feet!
              COLOR   ADJECTIVE

- **Thoroughbred:** You're a/an _____ and you _____ it.
                                   OCCUPATION   VERB

  Born to run like the _____ , some call you _____-
                           NOUN   ADJECTIVE

  blooded. But they're just jealous of your _____-star vibe.
                                               NOUN

- _____ **Pony:** You're sturdy on your _____ and
     A PLACE   PART OF THE BODY

  _____ for your size. Known for your high _____ , you
    ADJECTIVE   NOUN

  get into _____ when you're bored or don't _____ your
              NOUN   VERB

  way.

MAD LIBS® is fun to play with friends, but you can also play it by yourself! To begin with, DO NOT look at the story on the page below. Fill in the blanks on this page with the words called for. Then, using the words you have selected, fill in the blank spaces in the story.

Now you've created your own hilarious MAD LIBS® game!

WILD AS THE WIND

VERB (PAST TENSE) _____

VEHICLE _____

VERB (PAST TENSE) _____

A PLACE _____

PLURAL NOUN _____

ADJECTIVE _____

NUMBER _____

PLURAL NOUN _____

TYPE OF FOOD (PLURAL) _____

OCCUPATION (PLURAL) _____

ANIMAL _____

VERB _____

VERB (PAST TENSE) _____

ANIMAL _____

PLURAL NOUN _____

NOUN _____

ADJECTIVE _____

The story of how ponies arrived on Assateague Island sounds

_____-up, but some believe it's true. According to legend,
VERB (PAST TENSE)

sometime in the 1600s, a Spanish _____ with a cargo of horses
VEHICLE

_____ near the coast of (the) _____. Some of the
VERB (PAST TENSE)   A PLACE

horses swam to the _____ of Assateague, where they have roamed
PLURAL NOUN

_____ ever since. Around _____ ponies still populate
ADJECTIVE   NUMBER

the island. To survive, they eat dune grass, _____, and wild
PLURAL NOUN

_____. Now, once a year, the ponies are rounded up by
TYPE OF FOOD (PLURAL)

_____ from the local fire department for the Annual
OCCUPATION (PLURAL)

_____ Swim. The ponies _____ across the channel to
ANIMAL   VERB

nearby Chincoteague Island, where some of the foals are _____
                                                         VERB (PAST TENSE)

at auction. This keeps the _____ population on Assateague Island
                           ANIMAL

manageable. After a few _____, the remaining ponies swim back to
                        PLURAL NOUN

their _____, free to be _____ as the wind until next year.
      NOUN   ADJECTIVE

MAD LIBS® is fun to play with friends, but you can also play it by yourself! To begin with, DO NOT look at the story on the page below. Fill in the blanks on this page with the words called for. Then, using the words you have selected, fill in the blank spaces in the story.

Now you've created your own hilarious MAD LIBS® game!

ENGLISH OR WESTERN?

ADJECTIVE _____

VERB ENDING IN "S" _____

ADJECTIVE _____

PART OF THE BODY _____

EXCLAMATION _____

VERB _____

ADJECTIVE _____

PART OF THE BODY _____

VERB ENDING IN "ING" _____

NOUN _____

VERB _____

ARTICLE OF CLOTHING (PLURAL) _____

ADJECTIVE _____

OCCUPATION _____

VERB (PAST TENSE) _____

VERB ENDING IN "ING" _____

MAD LIBS®
ENGLISH OR WESTERN?

Western and English are the most _____ types of horse riding. Take
<u>ADJECTIVE</u>

the quiz to find out which style best _____ you.
<u>VERB ENDING IN "S"</u>

1. Do you like to: (a) relax in a/an _____ saddle and use only one
<u>ADJECTIVE</u>

_____ to hold the reins? (_____ , those selfies aren't
<u>PART OF THE BODY</u>   <u>EXCLAMATION</u>

going to _____ themselves!) Or do you: (b) prefer a light,
<u>VERB</u>

_____ saddle so you can have close contact with your horse's
<u>ADJECTIVE</u>

_____ ?
<u>PART OF THE BODY</u>

2. Do you: (a) keep things casual by _____ jeans and
<u>VERB ENDING IN "ING"</u>

a cowboy _____ when you _____ your horse?
<u>NOUN</u>   <u>VERB</u>

Or do you: (b) make a habit of looking polished in your tall

_____ and _____ hunt cap?
<u>ARTICLE OF CLOTHING (PLURAL)</u>   <u>ADJECTIVE</u>

If you answered *a* to both questions, you're a Western _____ ,
<u>OCCUPATION</u>

partner. If you _____ *b* to both questions, mount up
<u>VERB (PAST TENSE)</u>

for some English _____ fun!
<u>VERB ENDING IN "ING"</u>

MAD LIBS® is fun to play with friends, but you can also play it by yourself! To begin with, DO NOT look at the story on the page below. Fill in the blanks on this page with the words called for. Then, using the words you have selected, fill in the blank spaces in the story.

Now you've created your own hilarious MAD LIBS® game!

PONY EXPRESS

VERB (PAST TENSE)_____

PLURAL NOUN_____

NUMBER_____

PART OF THE BODY_____

ANIMAL_____

ADJECTIVE_____

VERB_____

ADVERB_____

NUMBER_____

VERB (PAST TENSE)_____

NOUN_____

NOUN_____

ADJECTIVE_____

ADJECTIVE_____

OCCUPATION (PLURAL)_____

VERB_____

ADJECTIVE_____

The pony express was a mail service that, from 1860 to 1861, _____
_____ (VERB (PAST TENSE)) letters and _____ (PLURAL NOUN) to settlers on the West Coast. Customers paid

around five dollars to send a letter (that's nearly _____ (NUMBER) dollars in today's

money!), which was _____ (PART OF THE BODY) -carried over 1,800 miles by a relay of

riders on _____ (ANIMAL) -back. These _____ (ADJECTIVE) riders galloped day

and night to _____ (VERB) their leg of the journey as _____ (ADVERB) as

possible. Sometimes they rode for _____ (NUMBER) hours at a time! Their mail

pouches—or mochilas—were then _____ (VERB (PAST TENSE)) off to a fresh horse

and rider team to carry the _____ (NOUN) for the rest of its journey. Because

their _____ (NOUN) was so _____ (ADJECTIVE), pony express riders earned

a lot of money. A famous advertisement for riders read "Wanted: Young,

_____ (ADJECTIVE), lightweight fellows not over eighteen. Must be expert

_____ (OCCUPATION (PLURAL)), willing to _____ (VERB) death daily. Orphans

preferred." Would you have been _____ (ADJECTIVE) enough to ride for the pony

express?

MAD LIBS® is fun to play with friends, but you can also play it by yourself! To begin with, DO NOT look at the story on the page below. Fill in the blanks on this page with the words called for. Then, using the words you have selected, fill in the blank spaces in the story.

Now you've created your own hilarious MAD LIBS® game!

THE MANE EVENT

NUMBER _____

EVENT _____

ADJECTIVE _____

TYPE OF LIQUID _____

PART OF THE BODY _____

NOUN _____

VERB ENDING IN "ING" _____

PART OF THE BODY (PLURAL) _____

ADVERB _____

VERB _____

VERB _____

NOUN _____

VERB _____

OCCUPATION _____

NOUN _____

VERB ENDING IN "ING" _____

MAD LIBS®
THE MANE EVENT

Master horseman Manuel has been competing since he was _____

<u>NUMBER</u>

years old and knows what it takes to get his mount sparkling clean before a big

_____ . He always gives his horse a bath with _____ water

<u>EVENT</u>   <u>ADJECTIVE</u>

and uses quality shampoo and _____ on her coat, mane, and

<u>TYPE OF LIQUID</u>

_____ . Once she's clean, Manuel covers his horse with a/an

<u>PART OF THE BODY</u>

_____ so she doesn't get chilly. He dries her off thoroughly,

<u>NOUN</u>

_____ from ears to _____ . Then he

<u>VERB ENDING IN "ING"</u>   <u>PART OF THE BODY (PLURAL)</u>

brushes out her mane and tail _____ with a/an _____ -comb. If

<u>ADVERB</u>   <u>VERB</u>

he hits a stubborn tangle, Manuel makes sure not to _____ on it!

<u>VERB</u>

Instead, he sprays a little _____ on the knot to work it loose. Finally,

<u>NOUN</u>

Manuel always remembers to _____ his horse's hooves. Though she

<u>VERB</u>

already looks as fancy as a/an _____ , he gives her hooves a little

<u>OCCUPATION</u>

extra _____ by _____ them with shoe polish.

<u>NOUN</u>   <u>VERB ENDING IN "ING"</u>

MAD LIBS® is fun to play with friends, but you can also play it by yourself! To begin with, DO NOT look at the story on the page below. Fill in the blanks on this page with the words called for. Then, using the words you have selected, fill in the blank spaces in the story.

Now you've created your own hilarious MAD LIBS® game!

HORSE TRIVIA

ADJECTIVE _____

VERB _____

NUMBER _____

ANIMAL (PLURAL) _____

NOUN _____

VERB _____

EXCLAMATION _____

NUMBER _____

ADJECTIVE _____

OCCUPATION (PLURAL) _____

VERB (PAST TENSE) _____

PART OF THE BODY _____

ADJECTIVE _____

NOUN _____

PART OF THE BODY (PLURAL) _____

MAD LIBS
HORSE TRIVIA

Time for some _____ horse trivia!
ADJECTIVE

• Horses learn to _____ about _____ hours after their
  VERB   NUMBER
  birth. Wild horses were hunted by _____, so newborn foals have
                                    ANIMAL (PLURAL)
  the natural _____ to get up and go rather quickly. Horses are
              NOUN
  literally born to _____. _____!
                    VERB   EXCLAMATION

• Most horses live between twenty and _____ years. Many
                                      NUMBER
  domesticated horses have long and _____ life spans if they are fed
                                    ADJECTIVE
  well and cared for by their _____.
                              OCCUPATION (PLURAL)

• The height of a horse is _____ in units called hands.
                           VERB (PAST TENSE)
  One hand is equal to four inches—the approximate width of a man's
  _____. This way of measuring dates back to the
  PART OF THE BODY
  _____ Egyptians and is still used today. A horse's _____ is
  ADJECTIVE   NOUN
  measured from the bottom of its _____ up to its
                                  PART OF THE BODY (PLURAL)
  withers, or shoulders.

MAD LIBS® is fun to play with friends, but you can also play it by yourself! To begin with, DO NOT look at the story on the page below. Fill in the blanks on this page with the words called for. Then, using the words you have selected, fill in the blank spaces in the story.

Now you've created your own hilarious MAD LIBS® game!

EQUINE ATHLETES

ADJECTIVE _____

ADVERB _____

VERB _____

NOUN _____

VERB _____

VERB ENDING IN "ING" _____

PLURAL NOUN _____

VERB ENDING IN "ING" _____

ADJECTIVE _____

VERB _____

PLURAL NOUN _____

PART OF THE BODY _____

NOUN _____

NUMBER _____

COLOR _____

MAD LIBS
EQUINE ATHLETES

"Faster, higher, _____!" The Olympic motto _____
            ADJECTIVE   ADVERB

embodies the horses and athletes that _____ together in the games.
                                       VERB

Like several other competitions, equestrian events are a/an _____
                                                  NOUN

where women and men _____ equally. There are three Olympic
                            VERB

events featuring horse-and-rider teams: Dressage, Eventing, and the

heart-_____ drama of Show Jumping. Dressage requires
          VERB ENDING IN "ING"

horses to carry their riders through a series of gaits, shapes, and _____.
                                                PLURAL NOUN

It's like _____ a ballet on horseback. Eventing is a/an
           VERB ENDING IN "ING"

_____ test of skill. Horses must _____ over or go through
        ADJECTIVE   VERB

approximately forty _____ on an outdoor course. Show Jumping is
                           PLURAL NOUN

the most _____-popping Olympic equestrian event. Riders take
              PART OF THE BODY

their horses over a series of _____-made obstacles while the crowd
                            NOUN

watches in suspense. Some of the jumps are up to _____ feet tall. It's
                                              NUMBER

a/an _____-medal-worthy spectacle!
     COLOR

MAD LIBS®

PETS-A-PALOOZA
MAD LIBS

by Anu Ohioma

INSTRUCTIONS

MAD LIBS® is a game for people who don't like games!
It can be played by one, two, three, four, or forty.

• RIDICULOUSLY SIMPLE DIRECTIONS

In this tablet you will find stories containing blank spaces where words are left out. One player, the READER, selects one of these stories. The READER does not tell anyone what the story is about. Instead, he/she asks the other players, the WRITERS, to give him/her words. These words are used to fill in the blank spaces in the story.

• TO PLAY

The READER asks each WRITER in turn to call out a word—an adjective or a noun or whatever the space calls for—and uses them to fill in the blank spaces in the story. The result is a MAD LIBS® game.

When the READER then reads the completed MAD LIBS® game to the other players, they will discover that they have written a story that is fantastic, screamingly funny, shocking, silly, crazy, or just plain dumb—depending upon which words each WRITER called out.

• EXAMPLE (*Before* and *After*)

"_____!" he said _____
       EXCLAMATION   ADVERB

as he jumped into his convertible _____ and
                                          NOUN

drove off with his _____ wife.
                         ADJECTIVE

"_____OUCH_____!" he said _____HAPPILY_____
       EXCLAMATION   ADVERB

as he jumped into his convertible _____CAT_____ and
                                          NOUN

drove off with his _____BRAVE_____ wife.
                         ADJECTIVE

MAD LIBS®

QUICK REVIEW

In case you have forgotten what adjectives, adverbs, nouns, and verbs are, here is a quick review:

An ADJECTIVE describes something or somebody. *Lumpy, soft, ugly, messy,* and *short* are adjectives.

An ADVERB tells how something is done. It modifies a verb and usually ends in "ly." *Modestly, stupidly, greedily,* and *carefully* are adverbs.

A NOUN is the name of a person, place, or thing. *Sidewalk, umbrella, bridle, bathtub,* and *nose* are nouns.

A VERB is an action word. *Run, pitch, jump,* and *swim* are verbs. Put the verbs in past tense if the directions say PAST TENSE. *Ran, pitched, jumped,* and *swam* are verbs in the past tense.

When we ask for A PLACE, we mean any sort of place: a country or city *(Spain, Cleveland)* or a room *(bathroom, kitchen).*

An EXCLAMATION or SILLY WORD is any sort of funny sound, gasp, grunt, or outcry, like *Wow!, Ouch!, Whomp!, Ick!,* and *Gadzooks!*

When we ask for specific words, like a NUMBER, a COLOR, an ANIMAL, or a PART OF THE BODY, we mean a word that is one of those things, like *seven, blue, horse,* or *head.*

When we ask for a PLURAL, it means more than one. For example, *cat* pluralized is *cats.*

MAD LIBS® is fun to play with friends, but you can also play it by yourself! To begin with, DO NOT look at the story on the page below. Fill in the blanks on this page with the words called for. Then, using the words you have selected, fill in the blank spaces in the story.

Now you've created your own hilarious MAD LIBS® game!

SO, YOU WANNA GET A PET?

VERB _____

NOUN _____

SILLY WORD _____

SAME SILLY WORD _____

ANIMAL _____

ANIMAL _____

NUMBER _____

ADJECTIVE _____

NOUN _____

ADJECTIVE _____

SOMETHING ALIVE _____

PLURAL NOUN _____

VERB _____

PART OF THE BODY _____

ADJECTIVE _____

PLURAL NOUN _____

NOUN _____

NOUN _____

If you _____ pets like I do, then you probably spend hours scrolling
      VERB

through pictures of them on Insta-_____ . And like me, you probably
      NOUN

go goo-goo _____-_____ over every _____ and
     SILLY WORD   SAME SILLY WORD   ANIMAL

_____ that pops up on your screen! Nearly _____ percent
   ANIMAL   NUMBER

of homes in America have at least one pet, so I can see why you'd want one.

After all, owning a pet helps you stay physically _____ and can
                                ADJECTIVE

improve your emotional _____ . Plus, pets are just so _____ !
              NOUN   ADJECTIVE

But being a good parent to a/an _____ can also be challenging.
                       SOMETHING ALIVE

You'll need to take your pet for _____, _____ for their
                   PLURAL NOUN   VERB

health care, and hold your _____ closed while you clean out their
               PART OF THE BODY

_____ _____ . But, in the end, their unconditional
 ADJECTIVE   PLURAL NOUN

_____ makes all the hard _____ totally worth it!
  NOUN   NOUN

MAD LIBS® is fun to play with friends, but you can also play it by yourself! To begin with, DO NOT look at the story on the page below. Fill in the blanks on this page with the words called for. Then, using the words you have selected, fill in the blank spaces in the story.

Now you've created your own hilarious MAD LIBS® game!

PROMISE TO MY PET

PERSON IN ROOM _____

CELEBRITY _____

ANIMAL _____

NOUN _____

ADJECTIVE _____

PLURAL NOUN _____

TYPE OF CONTAINER _____

TYPE OF LIQUID _____

ADJECTIVE _____

NOUN _____

VERB _____

PLURAL NOUN _____

NUMBER _____

PART OF THE BODY (PLURAL) _____

NOUN _____

VERB _____

A PLACE _____

VERB _____

MAD LIBS®
PROMISE TO MY PET

I, _____ , know that having a pet is a huge responsibility, so I
   PERSON IN ROOM

promise to give _____ , my pet _____ , all the love and
      CELEBRITY   ANIMAL

_____ he needs every day. I will remember to:
  NOUN

- Make sure he always feels _____ by giving him lots of snuggles
                    ADJECTIVE

  and _____ on his forehead
     PLURAL NOUN

- Feed him meals in his favorite _____ and fill his bowl with
                  TYPE OF CONTAINER

  _____ , so he's never hungry or _____
  TYPE OF LIQUID   ADJECTIVE

- Give him a cozy _____ to _____ in when he's tired
             NOUN   VERB

  and wash his _____ _____ times a week
       PLURAL NOUN   NUMBER

- Brush his _____ so he doesn't have bad _____
      PART OF THE BODY (PLURAL)   NOUN

- Take him outside to _____ around in (the) _____
             VERB   A PLACE

  so he doesn't _____ in the house
      VERB

MAD LIBS® is fun to play with friends, but you can also play it by yourself! To begin with, DO NOT look at the story on the page below. Fill in the blanks on this page with the words called for. Then, using the words you have selected, fill in the blank spaces in the story.

Now you've created your own hilarious MAD LIBS® game!

TURTLE TALK

TYPE OF BUILDING _____

VERB _____

SOMETHING ALIVE (PLURAL) _____

ADJECTIVE _____

VERB (PAST TENSE) _____

PLURAL NOUN _____

PLURAL NOUN _____

TYPE OF FOOD _____

PART OF THE BODY (PLURAL) _____

ADJECTIVE _____

PLURAL NOUN _____

ADJECTIVE _____

VERB _____

PART OF THE BODY _____

NUMBER _____

NOUN _____

VERB _____

EXCLAMATION _____

MAD LIBS
TURTLE TALK

When people come to the pet _____, they usually
(TYPE OF BUILDING)

_____ past us reptiles on their way to the dogs and
(VERB)

_____ . But today is going to be my _____ day!
(SOMETHING ALIVE (PLURAL)) _(ADJECTIVE)_

Before going to sleep last night, I _____ my shell to make sure I
(VERB (PAST TENSE))

don't have any _____ on it. I've been lifting the _____ in
(PLURAL NOUN) _(PLURAL NOUN)_

my tank and eating nothing but _____ for the past week so my
(TYPE OF FOOD)

_____ will look totally _____ . I'm even
(PART OF THE BODY (PLURAL)) _(ADJECTIVE)_

giving off positive _____ all morning, so I'll be _____
(PLURAL NOUN) _(ADJECTIVE)_

when my new family comes to _____ in my tank. Nobody wants a
(VERB)

turtle who hides her _____ , legs, and tail in her shell! It's a few
(PART OF THE BODY)

minutes before _____ o'clock, and the doors will open soon. Time to
(NUMBER)

take one last deep _____ before someone special says to me, "You're
(NOUN)

the one I _____ !" and brings me to my new home. _____ !
(VERB) _(EXCLAMATION)_

MAD LIBS® is fun to play with friends, but you can also play it by yourself! To begin with, DO NOT look at the story on the page below. Fill in the blanks on this page with the words called for. Then, using the words you have selected, fill in the blank spaces in the story.

Now you've created your own hilarious MAD LIBS® game!

CONVERSATION ABOUT A PARAKEET

VERB ENDING IN "ING" _____

ADJECTIVE _____

NOUN _____

COLOR _____

NOUN _____

NOUN _____

ADJECTIVE _____

TYPE OF FOOD _____

VERB _____

ADJECTIVE _____

CELEBRITY _____

VERB _____

ADJECTIVE _____

VERB _____

EXCLAMATION _____

PERSON IN ROOM _____

ADJECTIVE _____

Daughter: I love _____ with my new parakeet, Mom! But I

VERB ENDING IN "ING"

don't know what to name her.

Mom: Oh! I've got some _____ ideas! Why not name her

ADJECTIVE

"_____," since she's as _____ as a/an _____?

NOUN ... COLOR ... NOUN

Or maybe name her "_____" because she's _____ like

NOUN ... ADJECTIVE

_____?

TYPE OF FOOD

Daughter: I _____ her a lot and she's pretty _____, so I

VERB ... ADJECTIVE

don't think those names match her personality.

Mom: Maybe you can name her "_____" because they both love to

CELEBRITY

_____?

VERB

Daughter: I think that's a/an _____ idea, but it's still not quite right.

ADJECTIVE

Mom: Do you want to take a break and _____ about it later?

VERB

Daughter: _____! I've got it! I'll name her _____

EXCLAMATION ... PERSON IN ROOM

because she's so kind and _____, just like you!

ADJECTIVE

MAD LIBS® is fun to play with friends, but you can also play it by yourself! To begin with, DO NOT look at the story on the page below. Fill in the blanks on this page with the words called for. Then, using the words you have selected, fill in the blank spaces in the story.

Now you've created your own hilarious MAD LIBS® game!

POEM FOR A FERRET

PART OF THE BODY (PLURAL) _____

ADJECTIVE _____

ADJECTIVE _____

VERB ENDING IN "ING" _____

VERB ENDING IN "ING" _____

PART OF THE BODY (PLURAL) _____

ADJECTIVE _____

NOUN _____

TYPE OF FOOD _____

ADJECTIVE _____

NOUN _____

ADJECTIVE _____

ADJECTIVE _____

VERB _____

PART OF THE BODY (PLURAL) _____

NOUN _____

NOUN _____

PART OF THE BODY _____

MAD LIBS
POEM FOR A FERRET

With their lean _____ and their
_____ **PART OF THE BODY (PLURAL)**

_____ natures,
ADJECTIVE

ferrets are very _____ players.
ADJECTIVE

_____ high and _____ low,
VERB ENDING IN "ING"   **VERB ENDING IN "ING"**

they wiggle their _____ as they run to and fro.
PART OF THE BODY (PLURAL)

In Latin their name means "_____ thief."
ADJECTIVE

They're _____ eaters who love a good _____ leaf.
NOUN   **TYPE OF FOOD**

Although ferrets are _____ and can't see far,
ADJECTIVE

their sense of _____ is _____ and way above par.
NOUN   **ADJECTIVE**

When ferrets get _____ , they love to dance.
ADJECTIVE

They _____ their _____ like they're in
VERB   **PART OF THE BODY (PLURAL)**

a/an _____ .
NOUN

If you can give the _____ this pet requires,
NOUN

a ferret will fulfill your _____'s sweetest desires.
PART OF THE BODY

MAD LIBS® is fun to play with friends, but you can also play it by yourself! To begin with, DO NOT look at the story on the page below. Fill in the blanks on this page with the words called for. Then, using the words you have selected, fill in the blank spaces in the story.

Now you've created your own hilarious MAD LIBS® game!

DIARY ENTRY ABOUT MY KITTY

ADVERB _____

SOMETHING ALIVE _____

VERB ENDING IN "ING" _____

VERB ENDING IN "ING" _____

ANIMAL (PLURAL) _____

PART OF THE BODY (PLURAL) _____

ADJECTIVE _____

CELEBRITY _____

CELEBRITY _____

NUMBER _____

VERB (PAST TENSE) _____

PART OF THE BODY _____

NOUN _____

PART OF THE BODY (PLURAL) _____

COLOR _____

PLURAL NOUN _____

PLURAL NOUN _____

VERB _____

Dear Diary,

Guess what happened today? Dad _____ surprised me with a trip to
 ADVERB

the _____ shop! When we arrived, there were _____
 SOMETHING ALIVE   VERB ENDING IN "ING"

parrots to my left and _____ _____ to my right. It
 VERB ENDING IN "ING"   ANIMAL (PLURAL)

was overwhelming. But when I locked _____ with this one
 PART OF THE BODY (PLURAL)

_____ kitty, I knew she was going to be the _____ to my
 ADJECTIVE   CELEBRITY

_____. She let me pet her for _____ minutes straight! She
 CELEBRITY   NUMBER

even _____ her tail around my _____. My dad said it
 VERB (PAST TENSE)   PART OF THE BODY

was probably a coincidence that her furry _____ is the same color
 NOUN

as my _____: _____! But I don't believe in
 PART OF THE BODY (PLURAL) COLOR

_____. I took her for a stroll down the _____ just to
 PLURAL NOUN   PLURAL NOUN

confirm what I already knew . . . this kitty belonged to me. Dad let me bring

her home! The next thing I'm going to do is teach her how to _____!
                                                             VERB

MAD LIBS® is fun to play with friends, but you can also play it by yourself! To begin with, DO NOT look at the story on the page below. Fill in the blanks on this page with the words called for. Then, using the words you have selected, fill in the blank spaces in the story.

Now you've created your own hilarious MAD LIBS® game!

HOW TO TAKE CARE OF YOUR TARANTULA

PLURAL NOUN _____

NUMBER _____

VERB _____

VERB _____

NUMBER _____

ADJECTIVE _____

VERB _____

TYPE OF CONTAINER _____

VERB _____

VERB _____

ADJECTIVE _____

NOUN _____

ADJECTIVE _____

ADJECTIVE _____

ANIMAL (PLURAL) _____

VERB _____

VERB ENDING IN "ING" _____

MAD LIBS®
HOW TO TAKE CARE
OF YOUR TARANTULA

Tarantulas make great _____! These _____-legged
                         PLURAL NOUN   NUMBER
critters are interesting to _____ and can _____ for up
                                  VERB   VERB
to _____ years. They're easy to take care of if you follow these
      NUMBER
_____ tips.
   ADJECTIVE

- Tarantulas love to _____ , so keep the top of the _____
                          VERB   TYPE OF CONTAINER
  locked tight.

- Look, don't _____! Tarantulas can _____ with
                   VERB   VERB
  their fangs.

- Since tarantulas are _____ creatures, keep their tanks away
                            ADJECTIVE
  from your bright desktop _____ so they can get some
                                 NOUN
  _____ sleep during the day.
     ADJECTIVE

- Make sure your tarantulas have plenty of delicious crickets,
  _____-worms, and _____ to eat. Never _____ a
     ADJECTIVE   ANIMAL (PLURAL)   VERB
  tarantula when it is _____ .
                        VERB ENDING IN "ING"

MAD LIBS® is fun to play with friends, but you can also play it by yourself! To begin with, DO NOT look at the story on the page below. Fill in the blanks on this page with the words called for. Then, using the words you have selected, fill in the blank spaces in the story.

Now you've created your own hilarious MAD LIBS® game!

HAMSTER OR GERBIL?

CELEBRITY _____

PERSON IN ROOM _____

ADJECTIVE _____

PLURAL NOUN _____

VERB ENDING IN "ING" _____

TYPE OF FOOD (PLURAL) _____

ADJECTIVE _____

ADJECTIVE _____

PART OF THE BODY (PLURAL) _____

PART OF THE BODY _____

PART OF THE BODY (PLURAL) _____

SAME TYPE OF FOOD (PLURAL) _____

VERB _____

A PLACE _____

VERB ENDING IN "ING" _____

ADJECTIVE _____

PLURAL NOUN _____

VERB _____

At first glance, hamsters and gerbils look as similar as _____
CELEBRITY

and _____. They both have _____ ears and tiny
PERSON IN ROOM ADJECTIVE

_____ they use for _____. And they love to eat
PLURAL NOUN VERB ENDING IN "ING"

_____. But if you take a closer look, they're very different.
TYPE OF FOOD (PLURAL)

Hamsters are _____ all over. This includes their _____
ADJECTIVE ADJECTIVE

tails and cute _____. Gerbils, on the other
PART OF THE BODY (PLURAL)

_____, tend to be long and have roomy _____
PART OF THE BODY PART OF THE BODY (PLURAL)

where they store _____ they want to save for later. Since
SAME TYPE OF FOOD (PLURAL)

gerbils like to _____ together, they easily adapt to life in your
VERB

_____ and will make friends with other gerbils. But if two hamsters
A PLACE

are together, they might end up _____. You also don't want
VERB ENDING IN "ING"

to wake one up in the middle of the day because they can get really

_____. Now that you know the facts about both _____,
ADJECTIVE PLURAL NOUN

which one will you _____?
VERB

MAD LIBS® is fun to play with friends, but you can also play it by yourself! To begin with, DO NOT look at the story on the page below. Fill in the blanks on this page with the words called for. Then, using the words you have selected, fill in the blank spaces in the story.

Now you've created your own hilarious MAD LIBS® game!

SHOW-"ANT"-TELL!

VERB _____

ANIMAL _____

NUMBER _____

NUMBER _____

NOUN _____

VERB _____

PLURAL NOUN _____

ANIMAL (PLURAL) _____

VERB _____

NOUN _____

PERSON IN ROOM _____

CELEBRITY _____

VERB (PAST TENSE) _____

A PLACE _____

NOUN _____

VERB ENDING IN "ING" _____

NOUN _____

TYPE OF CONTAINER _____

MAD LIBS®
SHOW-"ANT"-TELL!

Teacher: Who wants to go next for show-and-_____?
_{VERB}

Student: I do! Here is my _____ farm! I started it when I was
_{ANIMAL}

_____ years old, and now I have over _____ ants. My ant farm
_{NUMBER}   _{NUMBER}

is made of _____ so we can _____ what's going on inside.
_{NOUN}   _{VERB}

I've watched my ants grow from tiny _____ to full-size
_{PLURAL NOUN}

_____ so many times I could _____ a/an
_{ANIMAL (PLURAL)}   _{VERB}

_____ about it. _____ and _____ are my
_{NOUN}   _{PERSON IN ROOM}   _{CELEBRITY}

favorite ants because I _____ them in (the) _____ by
_{VERB (PAST TENSE)}   _{A PLACE}

my grandmother's _____.
_{NOUN}

Teacher: Are you going to keep _____ to expand your
_{VERB ENDING IN "ING"}

collection?

Student: You bet your bottom _____ I am! I already have another
_{NOUN}

_____ filled with ants to bring in next week.
_{TYPE OF CONTAINER}

MAD LIBS® is fun to play with friends, but you can also play it by yourself! To begin with, DO NOT look at the story on the page below. Fill in the blanks on this page with the words called for. Then, using the words you have selected, fill in the blank spaces in the story.

Now you've created your own hilarious MAD LIBS® game!

PIGGING OUT!

ADJECTIVE _____

TYPE OF FOOD _____

ADJECTIVE _____

VERB ENDING IN "ING" _____

NUMBER _____

SAME TYPE OF FOOD _____

VERB ENDING IN "ING" _____

VERB _____

PLURAL NOUN _____

TYPE OF FOOD _____

ADJECTIVE _____

VERB _____

TYPE OF CONTAINER _____

ADJECTIVE _____

NOUN _____

VERB ENDING IN "ING" _____

ADJECTIVE _____

COLOR _____

MAD LIBS
PIGGING OUT!

Today I'm going to teach you how to make _____ _____
                                              ADJECTIVE   TYPE OF FOOD

that is _____ and nutritious for your pig! We'll start by
              ADJECTIVE

_____ _____ pounds of _____ vines and
VERB ENDING IN "ING"   NUMBER   SAME TYPE OF FOOD

_____ them out to dry in the sun. Then we'll _____
VERB ENDING IN "ING"   VERB

the vines into tiny _____ and mix them with twenty pounds of
                          PLURAL NOUN

_____ germ. Sprinkle one pound of _____ salt
   TYPE OF FOOD   ADJECTIVE

and _____ thoroughly. Pour the mixture into an airtight
          VERB

_____ and pack the vine pieces together tightly so the mix won't
TYPE OF CONTAINER

go _____. Store in a clean, dry area for at least three weeks, and
      ADJECTIVE

make sure it's not near direct _____-light or _____
                                      NOUN   VERB ENDING IN "ING"

water. Once it smells _____ and has turned _____, then
                            ADJECTIVE   COLOR

it's ready for your pig to eat!

MAD LIBS® is fun to play with friends, but you can also play it by yourself! To begin with, DO NOT look at the story on the page below. Fill in the blanks on this page with the words called for. Then, using the words you have selected, fill in the blank spaces in the story.

Now you've created your own hilarious MAD LIBS® game!

FISHY'S NEW HOME

SILLY WORD _____

ADJECTIVE _____

TYPE OF CONTAINER _____

ADJECTIVE _____

VERB (PAST TENSE) _____

NUMBER _____

PLURAL NOUN _____

NUMBER _____

TYPE OF LIQUID _____

PLURAL NOUN _____

VERB _____

NUMBER _____

NOUN _____

ADVERB _____

NOUN _____

TYPE OF FOOD _____

ADJECTIVE _____

VERB _____

MAD LIBS®
FISHY'S NEW HOME

_____, little fishy! I hope you're _____ in your new home.
    SILLY WORD   ADJECTIVE

I cleaned the inside of your _____ with a non-_____
                              TYPE OF CONTAINER   ADJECTIVE

sponge and placed the tank far away from the window. We wouldn't want you

getting sun-_____. I also put _____ pounds of
              VERB (PAST TENSE)   NUMBER

_____ and _____ gallons of _____ into your tank.
  PLURAL NOUN   NUMBER   TYPE OF LIQUID

Then I decorated it with plenty of _____ for you to _____
                                    PLURAL NOUN   VERB

around. And you don't have to worry about having clean water because I've also

installed a/an _____-stage _____ system. The first thing I'll
               NUMBER   NOUN

do after I've _____ transported you to your new home is treat you to
              ADVERB

a healthy _____! Your choices are _____ flakes or
          NOUN   TYPE OF FOOD

a/an _____ piece of zucchini. So, which would you like to
        ADJECTIVE

_____?
  VERB

MAD LIBS® is fun to play with friends, but you can also play it by yourself! To begin with, DO NOT look at the story on the page below. Fill in the blanks on this page with the words called for. Then, using the words you have selected, fill in the blank spaces in the story.

Now you've created your own hilarious MAD LIBS® game!

THE NEW CHICKS ON THE BLOCK

VERB _____

ADJECTIVE _____

TYPE OF CONTAINER _____

NUMBER _____

TYPE OF FOOD (PLURAL) _____

VERB _____

ADJECTIVE _____

PERSON IN ROOM _____

SILLY WORD _____

SILLY WORD _____

ADVERB _____

SOMETHING ALIVE _____

TYPE OF BUILDING _____

ANIMAL (PLURAL) _____

EXCLAMATION _____

NOUN _____

VERB _____

MAD LIBS®
THE NEW CHICKS
ON THE BLOCK

Chick 1: I'm excited to _____ the rest of our _____
                              VERB   ADJECTIVE

brothers and sisters who just hatched in the heated _____.
                TYPE OF CONTAINER

There must be, like, _____ of them in there. That's a lot of
                    NUMBER

_____ for one chicken to lay!
TYPE OF FOOD (PLURAL)

Chick 2: I couldn't _____ with you more. Look at that
                         VERB

_____ one they call "_____." Or that one they call
ADJECTIVE   PERSON IN ROOM

"_____-_____"! She's _____ adorable,
SOMETHING ALIVE   SOMETHING ALIVE   ADVERB

too! Actually, they're all cuter than a/an _____ in a/an
                                    SOMETHING ALIVE

_____.
TYPE OF BUILDING

Chick 1: I know. All these baby _____ make me want to scream,
                        ANIMAL (PLURAL)

"_____!" There's only one _____ . . . how can we
EXCLAMATION   NOUN

_____ them apart?
VERB

MAD LIBS® is fun to play with friends, but you can also play it by yourself! To begin with, DO NOT look at the story on the page below. Fill in the blanks on this page with the words called for. Then, using the words you have selected, fill in the blank spaces in the story.

Now you've created your own hilarious MAD LIBS® game!

THE PERKS OF OLDER DOGS

ADJECTIVE _____

ANIMAL (PLURAL) _____

TYPE OF BUILDING _____

PLURAL NOUN _____

EXCLAMATION _____

OCCUPATION _____

PLURAL NOUN _____

NOUN _____

VERB _____

NOUN _____

VERB _____

VERB ENDING IN "ING" _____

PLURAL NOUN _____

VERB _____

TYPE OF FOOD _____

NUMBER _____

NOUN _____

COLOR _____

MAD LIBS®
THE PERKS OF OLDER DOGS

Adopting a puppy might be _____, but older _____
 ADJECTIVE ANIMAL (PLURAL)
are awesome, too. For instance, many of them have already been

_____-trained. That means there's no _____ to clean
 TYPE OF BUILDING PLURAL NOUN
up when you get home late from school because Mr. _____, your
 EXCLAMATION
_____, kept you after class to do extra math _____. Older
 OCCUPATION PLURAL NOUN
dogs are also very well behaved. They won't climb on your antique

_____ or _____ laps around the _____-room
 NOUN VERB NOUN
the moment you unlock the door. And they understand basic commands like

"sit," "stay," and "_____." This frees up time you'd normally
 VERB
spend _____ a puppy, so you can teach your old dog new
 VERB ENDING IN "ING"
_____ instead. But my favorite thing about older dogs is that they
 PLURAL NOUN
don't _____ if you want to stay home and be a couch _____
 VERB TYPE OF FOOD
for the evening . . . they know the joys of a/an _____-hour TV binge!
 NUMBER
So, while some say older dogs are over the _____, I say they're in
 NOUN
their _____ years!
 COLOR

MAD LIBS® is fun to play with friends, but you can also play it by yourself! To begin with, DO NOT look at the story on the page below. Fill in the blanks on this page with the words called for. Then, using the words you have selected, fill in the blank spaces in the story.

Now you've created your own hilarious MAD LIBS® game!

IT'S LLAMA TIME!

ADJECTIVE _____

VERB _____

ANIMAL (PLURAL) _____

ARTICLE OF CLOTHING _____

A PLACE _____

VERB _____

PART OF THE BODY _____

VERB ENDING IN "S" _____

PART OF THE BODY _____

TYPE OF FOOD _____

VERB _____

ADJECTIVE _____

A PLACE _____

PLURAL NOUN _____

NUMBER _____

PLURAL NOUN _____

ANIMAL _____

EXCLAMATION _____

MAD LIBS
IT'S LLAMA TIME!

You may not believe it, but you can actually adopt a/an _____ llama!
                                                         ADJECTIVE

All you need to do is _____ out of bed in the morning, slip on
                          VERB

your favorite "I love _____" _____, and get
                      ANIMAL (PLURAL)   ARTICLE OF CLOTHING

down to your local llama store in (the) _____. You don't even
                                          A PLACE

need to _____ your hair—llamas don't care about your new
            VERB

_____-style! Then, the excitement really _____
PART OF THE BODY   VERB ENDING IN "S"

when you and your llama come face-to-_____ for the first time.
                                      PART OF THE BODY

You feed them _____ and _____ them along the grass.
               TYPE OF FOOD   VERB

And that's it! You've got a new llama as your _____ friend. And since
                                               ADJECTIVE

no trip to (the) _____ is complete without a few free _____,
                  A PLACE   PLURAL NOUN

you'll also be leaving with a/an _____-inch llama made from recycled
                                  NUMBER

_____ (while supplies last) and a framed photo of your new
PLURAL NOUN

_____ . _____!
  ANIMAL   EXCLAMATION

MAD LIBS® is fun to play with friends, but you can also play it by yourself! To begin with, DO NOT look at the story on the page below. Fill in the blanks on this page with the words called for. Then, using the words you have selected, fill in the blank spaces in the story.

Now you've created your own hilarious MAD LIBS® game!

FIND MY BOA!

NOUN _____

PERSON IN ROOM _____

ADJECTIVE _____

ADJECTIVE _____

ADVERB _____

VERB _____

A PLACE _____

VERB _____

VERB _____

TYPE OF BUILDING _____

NOUN _____

PLURAL NOUN _____

PART OF THE BODY (PLURAL) _____

ADJECTIVE _____

VERB ENDING IN "ING" _____

VERB ENDING IN "ING" _____

NOUN _____

MAD LIBS®
FIND MY BOA!

Have no _____; _____, the Boa Finder, is here! Snakes
        NOUN   PERSON IN ROOM

are _____ animals who love to escape their tanks. But with these
     ADJECTIVE

_____ tips, you can find your snake _____.
   ADJECTIVE   ADVERB

- _____ where you last saw your boa by carefully searching
      VERB

  one _____ at a time. _____ like a snake to guess
      A PLACE   VERB

  where your boa would _____ after it escaped from your
                   VERB

  _____.
   TYPE OF BUILDING

- Use the _____ on your phone to take pictures of any nooks
        NOUN

  and _____ that are too small for you to see into with your
     PLURAL NOUN

  own two _____.
       PART OF THE BODY (PLURAL)

- If you can't find your snake the _____-fashioned way,
                    ADJECTIVE

  then find them by _____ a trap. To do this, try
          VERB ENDING IN "ING"

  _____ a/an _____ on the ground so the snake
  VERB ENDING IN "ING"   NOUN

  has to slither through it.

MAD LIBS® is fun to play with friends, but you can also play it by yourself! To begin with, DO NOT look at the story on the page below. Fill in the blanks on this page with the words called for. Then, using the words you have selected, fill in the blank spaces in the story.

Now you've created your own hilarious MAD LIBS® game!

JUMPING FOR JOY

VERB _____

PART OF THE BODY (PLURAL) _____

VERB _____

TYPE OF FOOD _____

ANIMAL _____

ADVERB _____

ADVERB _____

NUMBER _____

PART OF THE BODY _____

VERB _____

ADJECTIVE _____

SILLY WORD _____

NUMBER _____

OCCUPATION _____

COLOR _____

TYPE OF EVENT _____

MAD☺LIBS®
JUMPING FOR JOY

Just because pet frogs have to _____ in a tank doesn't mean they can't

VERB

stretch their _____ and jump once in a while! Follow these

PART OF THE BODY (PLURAL)

steps to train your frog to _____ high.

VERB

- Place some _____ near the end of a/an _____ baster.

TYPE OF FOOD / ANIMAL

  Then _____ draw the food into the baster to keep it

ADVERB

  _____ attached.

ADVERB

- Hold the food _____ inches above the frog's _____

NUMBER / PART OF THE BODY

  and wait for your frog to jump up and _____ on it! Your frog

VERB

  may make a/an _____ "_____" sound.

ADJECTIVE / SILLY WORD

- Repeat _____ times a day, raising the baster each time.

NUMBER

Your frog will learn to jump like an Olympic _____ who's about to

OCCUPATION

win a/an _____ medal at the next summer _____!

COLOR / TYPE OF EVENT

MAD LIBS® is fun to play with friends, but you can also play it by yourself! To begin with, DO NOT look at the story on the page below. Fill in the blanks on this page with the words called for. Then, using the words you have selected, fill in the blank spaces in the story.

Now you've created your own hilarious MAD LIBS® game!

LIZARD-SITTER NEEDED

NUMBER _____

TYPE OF FOOD _____

PERSON IN ROOM _____

ADJECTIVE _____

TYPE OF EVENT _____

COUNTRY _____

VEHICLE _____

ADJECTIVE _____

SOMETHING ALIVE (PLURAL) _____

NOUN _____

VERB _____

ADJECTIVE _____

PART OF THE BODY _____

NUMBER _____

OCCUPATION _____

ADJECTIVE _____

VERB _____

LETTER OF THE ALPHABET _____

MAD LIBS
LIZARD-SITTER NEEDED

Are you a pet-sitter over the age of _____? Do you want to earn
                                          NUMBER

some extra _____ money? Do you love chameleons named
                  TYPE OF FOOD

_____? If so, then I've got the _____ job for you! My
PERSON IN ROOM   ADJECTIVE

family is going to a/an _____ in _____ and they won't
                      TYPE OF EVENT   COUNTRY

let me take my chameleon on the _____. All you need to do is feed
                                   VEHICLE

her _____ _____ every day, make sure that her
      ADJECTIVE   SOMETHING ALIVE (PLURAL)

heat _____ doesn't burn out, and _____ with her so she
        NOUN   VERB

doesn't feel _____. Oh, and she loves to have her _____
        ADJECTIVE   PART OF THE BODY

scratched! I am willing to pay _____ dollars per day for a great
                            NUMBER

pet-_____ who can take _____ care of my adorable
    OCCUPATION   ADJECTIVE

and scaly baby. To apply for this job, please contact me directly at:

i-_____-reptiles@-_____-mail.com.
  VERB   LETTER OF THE ALPHABET

MAD LIBS® is fun to play with friends, but you can also play it by yourself! To begin with, DO NOT look at the story on the page below. Fill in the blanks on this page with the words called for. Then, using the words you have selected, fill in the blank spaces in the story.

Now you've created your own hilarious MAD LIBS® game!

GUINEA PIG FACTS

VERB _____

ANIMAL (PLURAL) _____

NUMBER _____

NUMBER _____

VERB ENDING IN "ING" _____

VERB _____

LETTER OF THE ALPHABET _____

ADJECTIVE _____

COUNTRY _____

NUMBER _____

ADJECTIVE _____

VERB _____

VERB _____

TYPE OF FOOD _____

NOUN _____

NOUN _____

NUMBER _____

MAD LIBS®
GUINEA PIG FACTS

_____ out these cool facts about guinea _____!
VERB   ANIMAL (PLURAL)

- Guinea pigs have _____ toes on their front feet, but _____
  NUMBER   NUMBER

on their back feet. Their teeth are constantly _____.
                                                VERB ENDING IN "ING"

Like humans, guinea pigs need to _____ lots of vitamin
                                  VERB

_____, because their bodies cannot produce this
LETTER OF THE ALPHABET

_____ nutritional supplement.
ADJECTIVE

- _____ pigs are very active. They can stay awake for up to
  COUNTRY

_____ hours a day. When young guinea pigs feel _____,
NUMBER   ADJECTIVE

they do a dance known as "_____-corning" where they
                          VERB

_____ up and down repeatedly like kernels of real _____.
VERB   TYPE OF FOOD

- A male guinea pig is called a/an _____ and a female is called
                                   NOUN

a/an _____. The oldest guinea pig lived for over _____
     NOUN   NUMBER

years!

MAD LIBS® is fun to play with friends, but you can also play it by yourself! To begin with, DO NOT look at the story on the page below. Fill in the blanks on this page with the words called for. Then, using the words you have selected, fill in the blank spaces in the story.

Now you've created your own hilarious MAD LIBS® game!

LOUD AND PROUD

ADJECTIVE _____

PLURAL NOUN _____

PART OF THE BODY (PLURAL) _____

ADJECTIVE _____

ANIMAL _____

VERB _____

VERB (PAST TENSE) _____

SILLY WORD _____

NOUN _____

TYPE OF BUILDING _____

SOMETHING ALIVE (PLURAL) _____

NUMBER _____

NOUN _____

VERB _____

PART OF THE BODY _____

NOUN _____

PLURAL NOUN _____

MAD LIBS
LOUD AND PROUD

Cockatoos are _____ pet birds. They are best known for the
            ADJECTIVE

_____ they display on the top of their _____. But
PLURAL NOUN   PART OF THE BODY (PLURAL)

did you know they are extremely _____, too? Their loud
                           ADJECTIVE

_____ calls, which they use to _____ with other nearby
ANIMAL   VERB

cockatoos, can be _____ up to a mile away! These talkative birds
           VERB (PAST TENSE)

squawk with a distinctive "_____" during early morning and at dusk,
            SILLY WORD

so they may not be the best _____ if you live in a crowded
            NOUN

_____ in a big city. Otherwise, your next-door
TYPE OF BUILDING

_____ are likely to complain. Cockatoos can also learn up
SOMETHING ALIVE (PLURAL)

to _____ words in their lifetime. They will say "Good _____"
   NUMBER   NOUN

to you when the sun rises and _____ to themselves all throughout
                     VERB

the day. If your _____ is set on getting a cockatoo, then you also
       PART OF THE BODY

might want to invest in a pair of _____ -canceling head- _____
                    NOUN   PLURAL NOUN

for your neighbors!

MAD LIBS® is fun to play with friends, but you can also play it by yourself! To begin with, DO NOT look at the story on the page below. Fill in the blanks on this page with the words called for. Then, using the words you have selected, fill in the blank spaces in the story.

Now you've created your own hilarious MAD LIBS® game!

THE HERMIT CRAB RACE IS ON!

SOMETHING ALIVE (PLURAL) _____

ANIMAL _____

ADJECTIVE _____

LAST NAME _____

NUMBER _____

OCCUPATION _____

NOUN _____

VERB _____

SAME LAST NAME _____

ADJECTIVE _____

PERSON IN ROOM _____

PART OF THE BODY _____

ADJECTIVE _____

PART OF THE BODY _____

SILLY WORD _____

SAME LAST NAME _____

VERB ENDING IN "ING" _____

NOUN _____

MAD LIBS®
THE HERMIT CRAB RACE IS ON!

Announcer 1: Welcome, ladies and _____ , to the fifth

SOMETHING ALIVE (PLURAL)

annual hermit _____ race! Today our champion, _____

ANIMAL ADJECTIVE

Shell _____ , will defend his title against _____ newcomers.

LAST NAME NUMBER

_____ **2:** The contestants are on the starting _____ in the

OCCUPATION NOUN

center of the circle. The first one to _____ outside the ring wins . . .

VERB

and the race is on!

Announcer 1: _____ is in the lead, but here comes _____

SAME LAST NAME ADJECTIVE

_____ right on his _____! The crowd gets

PERSON IN ROOM PART OF THE BODY

_____ as the two race _____-and-neck.

ADJECTIVE PART OF THE BODY

Announcer 2: And, _____ ! It's over! _____ takes the win

SILLY WORD SAME LAST NAME

by _____ his claw. What a/an _____!

VERB ENDING IN "ING" NOUN

MAD LIBS® is fun to play with friends, but you can also play it by yourself! To begin with, DO NOT look at the story on the page below. Fill in the blanks on this page with the words called for. Then, using the words you have selected, fill in the blank spaces in the story.

Now you've created your own hilarious MAD LIBS® game!

WHICH PET IS RIGHT FOR YOU?

VERB ENDING IN "ING" _____

VERB _____

NOUN _____

A PLACE _____

NOUN _____

NOUN _____

ADJECTIVE _____

NOUN _____

ADJECTIVE _____

NOUN _____

VERB _____

A PLACE _____

NOUN _____

PART OF THE BODY _____

ANIMAL _____

ADJECTIVE _____

ANIMAL _____

MAD LIBS®
WHICH PET IS RIGHT FOR YOU?

_____ a pet is a big decision. _____ this quiz to find
VERB ENDING IN "ING"   VERB

out which animal is best for you.

1. I would rather: (a) go cross- _____ skiing at a/an _____
                                 NOUN   A PLACE

   on the weekend, (b) relax on the _____ and read a romance
                                    NOUN

   _____
   NOUN

2. I like being: (a) loud and _____ like a/an _____,
                              ADJECTIVE   NOUN

   (b) quiet as a/an _____ _____
                     ADJECTIVE   NOUN

3. I like to: (a) play an epic game of hide-and- _____ in (the)
                                                 VERB

   _____, (b) cuddle under a fuzzy _____ that's tucked
   A PLACE   NOUN

   around my _____
             PART OF THE BODY

If you picked mostly *a*'s, you should consider getting a/an _____.
                                                            ANIMAL

Mostly *b*'s means you'll love a/an _____ pet like a/an _____.
                                   ADJECTIVE   ANIMAL

Download Mad Libs today!

stories on our apps!

creating wacky and wonderful

Join the millions of Mad Libs fans